Does social science influence social policy? This is a topic of perennial concern among students of politics, the economy, and other social institutions. In *Effective Social Science*, eight prominent social researchers offer first-hand descriptions of the impact of their work on government and corporate policy.

In their own words, these noted political scientists, economists, and sociologists—among them such influential scholars as James Coleman, Joseph Pechman, and Eli Ginzberg—tell us what it was like to become involved in the making of social policy. These rich personal narratives, derived from detailed interviews conducted by Bernard Barber (himself a veteran of the biomedical policy arena), illuminate the role of social science in diverse areas, including school desegregation, comprehensive income taxation, military manpower utilization, transportation deregulation, and the protection of privacy.

The patterns traced in this volume indicate that social science can influence policy, but only as part of a pluralistic, *political* process; effective social research requires advocacy as well as a conducive social and ideological climate For anyone curious about the relationship between social knowledge and social action, this book provides both striking illustration and fruitful analysis.

EFFECTIVE SOCIAL SCIENCE

Eight Cases in Economics,
Political Science,
and Sociology

BY THE SAME AUTHOR

Science and the Social Order, 1952

Social Stratification, 1957

European Social Class: Stability and Change, 1965
(edited with Elinor G. Barber)

Drugs and Society, 1967

L. J. Henderson on the Social System, 1970 (editor)

Stability and Social Change, 1971 (edited with Alex Inkeles)

*Research on Human Subjects: Problems of Social Control
in Medical Experimentation,* 1973 (with John J. Lally,
Julia Loughlin Makarushka, and Daniel Sullivan)

Medical Ethics and Social Change, 1978 (editor)

*"Mass Apathy" and Voluntary Social Participation
in the United States,* 1980

Informed Consent in Medical Therapy and Research, 1980

The Logic and Limits of Trust, 1983

EFFECTIVE SOCIAL SCIENCE

*Eight Cases in Economics,
Political Science,
and Sociology*

BERNARD BARBER

RUSSELL SAGE FOUNDATION
New York

The Russell Sage Foundation

The Russell Sage Foundation, one of the oldest of America's general purpose foundations, was established in 1907 by Mrs. Margaret Olivia Sage for "the improvement of social and living conditions in the United States." The Foundation seeks to fulfill this mandate by fostering the development and dissemination of knowledge about the political, social, and economic problems of America. It conducts research in the social sciences and public policy, and publishes books and pamphlets that derive from this research.

The Board of Trustees is responsible for oversight and the general policies of the Foundation, while administrative direction of the program and staff is vested in the President, assisted by the officers and staff. The President bears final responsibility for the decision to publish a manuscript as a Russell Sage Foundation book. In reaching a judgment on the competence, accuracy, and objectivity of each study, the President is advised by the staff and selected expert readers. The conclusions and interpretations in Russell Sage Foundation publications are those of the authors and not of the Foundation, its Trustees, or its staff. Publication by the Foundation, therefore, does not imply endorsement of the contents of the study.

Library of Congress Cataloging-in-Publication Data

Barber, Bernard.
   Effective social science.

   Bibliography: p.
   Includes index.
   1. Social sciences—Research. 2. Social policy.
3. Policy sciences. I. Title.
H62.B327 1987   300   87-23416
ISBN 0-87154-091-6

Text design: HUGUETTE FRANCO

10 9 8 7 6 5 4 3 2 1

For Elinor

Once Again,
and More to Come

Acknowledgment

It is a special pleasure to acknowledge the long and productive relationship that I have had with the Russell Sage Foundation during the last thirty-five years. That relationship may also be of general interest insofar as it recapitulates something of the changing character of the Foundation's programs and structure during the period.

In the early 1950s, when I first came to Columbia University, I was asked by Donald Young, president of the Foundation, to offer a doctoral seminar in sociology at the New York School of Social Work, now the Columbia University School of Social Work. The school was located in the Carnegie Mansion on upper Fifth Avenue, which now houses the Cooper-Hewitt Museum of the Smithsonian Institution. During that period Young was pursuing his innovative program of bringing the new substance and method of the academic social sciences to the practicing professions. Under the Foundation program valuable work had already begun in the law and in medicine. Young was asked by the distinguished economist Eveline Burns, of the School of Social Work's faculty, to underwrite the beginnings of a doctoral program for social work. After giving my seminar for two years, some of the members of which later became leaders in the field of social work, I was asked to join the school's faculty on a permanent basis as the director of a doctoral program. I was satisfied where I was and refused, but the doctoral program continued and is still a valuable part of the curriculum at the Columbia School of Social Work. Some of its doctoral candidates have been students in my sociology courses, and I have sat on School of Social Work doctoral orals and dissertation defenses.

In the early 1960s I attended, with great pleasure and profit, the informal lunch discussion meetings which Bert Brim, who succeeded Young as president of the Foundation, held in his office. Together with his very able staff and various visitors from the New York social science community and elsewhere, Brim conducted wonderful discussions of all kinds of social science concerns, intellectual and organizational. On one occasion, rather presciently for that time, Brim said that the subject of drugs was going to be one of most important policy problems for the future. When I told him that I had prepared for my file an outline of a book on drugs and society, he offered to provide a grant to make the writing of that book possible. After a couple of years doing other work, I was able to take up his offer and wrote *Drugs and Society,* which was published by the Foundation in 1967.

In *Drugs and Society* I wrote a chapter on the ethics of biomedical researchers, especially in regard to the use of human subjects in bio-medical experimentation. That chapter was later published separately as an article in *The Public Interest* at the request of one of its editors, Daniel Bell, who was then one of my colleagues at Columbia. The topic of that chapter was to become not only a major public policy issue after the 1960s but also one of my own continuing research and policy inter-ests. The detailed story of those continuing interests is told in the ap-pendix of this book.

After the 1973 publication of *Research on Human Subjects: Problems of Social Control in Medical Experimentation* and after my involvement in a variety of policy activities connected with its subject, I hoped, as a sociologist of science, to describe my experience as a detailed case of what all social scientists are interested in, namely, the relation between empirical social research and social policy. I thought a book containing my case and a series of other social science cases would be useful for the social science community and for policy-makers. In the early 1980s, my work schedule finally making it possible, I applied to the new heads of the Russell Sage Foundation, President Marshall Robinson and Vice President Peter de Janosi, for a grant to do the book. The Foundation's program now emphasized work at the Foundation itself and I was in-vited to have a year in residence as a Senior Scholar. This book is the result. But more than the book resulted. My companions in residence— other Senior Scholars, Resident Scholars, Post-Doctoral Fellows, and staff—were good teachers; their assistance was valuable not only for this book but for many other intellectual interests.

Besides help for this book from the Russell Sage Foundation, it is a pleasure to acknowledge debts, moral and intellectual, to some friends-and-colleagues. Jeffrey Alexander, Jonathan Cole, and Viviana Zelizer are "trusted assessors" from whom I always ask and get good judgments not only on projects like this book but on other matters as well. Finally, as always for the last forty years, I have an immeasurably large debt, for moral support and intellectual guidance, to my wife, Elinor Barber.

New York City
Spring, 1987

Contents

Chapter One

Problem, Purpose, Plan

The effectiveness of social science knowledge—that is, the questions of *whether* it is useful or not and *how* it may be useful for social action and social policy—has been of perennial and widespread concern among social thinkers and social scientists. This concern goes back to the origins of systematic social knowledge among the Greek philosophers, continues through the preprofessional and prototypical modes of social thought of early modern times, and increases greatly as something called social science emerges and becomes institutionalized and professionalized. As the social sciences claim a place in the university, government, and business worlds of modern times, and as they seek solid legitimacy and establishment in those worlds, they are often asked by those already established and by funding agencies, and so they have to ask themselves, what is the use of what social scientists do? Is their knowledge effective and valuable? If we social scientists think so, how do we demonstrate effectiveness as a fact?

Sources of Concern About Effectiveness

Inside and outside modern social science there are several sources of this concern about effectiveness that are worth considering for the light they may shed on how and why the social scientists deal with the problem.

The Search for Legitimacy and Resources, Both Moral and Material

All emerging sciences seeking places as recognized disciplines in the modern university, wanting public visibility and legitimacy as well, have a continuing need to justify themselves. Hoping to claim a share of public and private funds for research from government, business, and the foundations, they are always implicitly or explicitly in competition with the established natural sciences and humanities for resources of talent, facilities, and money. The social sciences today have a need to demonstrate both their scientific character and their usefulness for so-cial policy and for social thought more generally. The social sciences have been preoccupied with the nature of science in general and with the particular ways in which they can call themselves scientific. It is by now taken for granted that the natural sciences are indeed both scien-tific and useful. Therefore, as the social sciences try to follow the scien-tific fields that have preceded them into legitimate and established status, they also stress both their scientific character and their useful-ness.

Science as Pure versus Science as Useful

Although legitimacy is contingent on being both scientific and useful, there is always some tension, in all the sciences, natural and social, be-tween the claim to be pure science and the claim to be useful. A care-ful balance must be struck to avoid losing legitimacy on one score or the other. Specialization of activities and purposes reduces this tension somewhat, but since the boundary line between basic or pure science and applied science is often vague and changing, there is a constant need, especially in the insecure social science disciplines, to justify each kind of work. Two classics in sociology illustrate this dual need for self-justification. At the turn of the century, Émile Durkheim, in *The Rules of Sociological Method,* in insisting on the existence of "social facts," was making an early claim to the scientific character of sociology. And some forty years later, Robert S. Lynd, in *Knowledge for What?,*[1] preached the need for social science to be useful. Lynd says that "social science is not

[1] Princeton University Press, 1939.

a scholarly arcanum but an organized part of the culture which exists to help man in continually understanding and rebuilding his culture." It is, he continues, "an instrument for furthering man's purposes . . ." (p. ix). Both Durkheim and Lynd have been inspirations for succeeding generations of sociologists and other social scientists. The tension between science for itself and science for usefulness heightens the felt need for justification in both respects. The ideal situation occurs when this tension can be resolved by claiming or showing that each of these two types of activities is necessary for the other's progress and achievements.

Scarcity of Resources

Science is always in competition with other desirable social and cultural activities for scarce resources. The greater such scarcity, the greater will be the tendency to claim usefulness, whether for the natural or the social sciences, as a basis for the "proper" allocation of these resources. The sciences claim usefulness in a number of different ways, direct and indirect. They may claim usefulness on the grounds that even pure science often, and especially eventually and in the long run, pays off in direct use, or that it is one of the essential sources for the development of applied research. Alternatively, they may point directly to the great success with which applied research has already been put to use. At all levels—in science overall, in broad groupings such as the social sciences, in particular established disciplines such as physics or chemistry, and even in specialties within disciplines—organized professional groups take as one of their essential purposes the preparation of systematic and detailed appeals for further and generally larger support. Such advocacy stresses both the quality and the utility and effectiveness of the work of the group making the appeal.

One of the most recent examples of such advocacy comes from physics, one of the most prestigious and recognizably useful of the natural sciences. A sixteen-member general committee took overall responsibility for the three-year justificatory project. A 184-page overview presented the committee's main findings. Seven supplements provided in-depth examination of various subfields of physics and of technological applications, each subfield reported on by a special panel from that area. Summing up, the news report about this effort in *Science,* the official journal of the American Association for the Advancement of Science, says, "in the end, the committee makes the probably true but nonetheless well-known argument that *the health of the American econ-*

omy depends in part on the ability of American physics to maintain a competitive edge relative to other countries. . . ."[2]

Studies of this seriousness and magnitude are not peculiar to physics. In recent years, as funds have become scarcer for research, studies have been produced by chemists and biologists as well. And also for the social sciences, although in their statement, the case must be made not only for their usefulness but for their scientific character. They are not yet fully established as sciences in the Congressional and public minds.

Cognitive Interest in the Problem of Usefulness

Unlike the natural sciences, the social sciences have a purely intellectual, cognitive interest in the nature of science and its consequences for social good and ill. In sociology especially, there have emerged such subspecialties as the sociology of science and the sociology of knowledge, which deal systematically with science and technology insofar as these have sources in and consequences for other parts of society. These sociological subspecialties, among their other tasks, seek to establish the interdependent relations between the sciences, including the social sciences, and their various useful technologies, and such other parts of the social system as the polity, the economy, the modes of communication, the arts, philosophy, and religion.

As long ago as 1949, Robert K. Merton, the founder of the sociology of sciences as a systematic discipline, recommended the serious study of applied social science, the ways in which social science is or can be useful and effective.[3] In this book I have chosen to act on that recommendation, building on my own earlier work in the sociology of science and knowledge, which began with *Science and the Social Order*[4] and which has continued since in a series of books and papers.

Value and Ideological Concerns

Because of society's need to cope effectively with the physical, biological, and social worlds, there is always some value placed on rationality and science for their own sake.[5] In our society we have developed elab-

---

[2] *Science* 232 (1986): 156. My italics.
[3] "The role of applied social science in the formation of policy," *Philosophy of Science,* 16 (July 1949):161–81.
[4] Glencoe, IL: Free Press, 1952.
[5] Bernard Barber, "Function, Variability, and Change in Ideological Systems," in Bernard Barber and Alex Inkeles, eds., *Stability and Social Change* (Boston: Little, Brown, 1971).

orate and powerful justificatory ideologies for this value. But other values and their associated ideologies stress the importance, indeed the indispensability, of the *instrumental effectiveness* of science for goals outside science itself: helping the poor and the ill, reducing inequality, eliminating crime, making government and other types of social organization more effective, and so on. Each of these ideologies seeks strength by producing evidence of the importance and validity of its claims. The search for such evidence overlaps with and is an important source of interest in the sociology of science and technology.

The Role of Outsiders

Advocacy emerges from justificatory pressures both internal and external to the sciences. Outsiders, the nonscientists, who often control resources, have other values, goals, interests, and purposes, and they want to know how these relate to those of science. As to social science specifically, they want to know *what* it is, *whether* it is "genuine" science, and *whether* it includes legitimate disciplines with a claim on scarce social resources. So, fairly and powerfully, these public outsiders ask: Are you a science? Are you useful at all? To whom are you useful? Social scientists recognize that they need to respond to these challenges and queries, partly to justify their claimed identity as a science, partly because outsiders are essential sources of moral and material support. For social scientists, this is another perennial and widespread concern about the relations between social science and social policy, between what they do and its effectiveness for social purposes.

For all these reasons, then, social scientists have been and will always be attentive to the problem on which this book tries to shed further light: the relationship between social research and social policy.

Previous Analysis of Effectiveness

Before proceeding further, we need to examine what is already known from past work about the effectiveness of social research. What is there to add to or build on?

Among the multitude of studies of the effectiveness of social science research, Carol Weiss's excellent work[6] provides a valuable reference

[6] *Social Science Research and Decision Making* (New York: Columbia University Press, 1980).

point for my own present work. As invaluable background and starting place for her empirical research on the processes of decision-making among middle-level executives in government mental health agencies, Weiss made an exhaustive survey and synthesis of what had previously been said about the relations between social science research and social policy by various commentators. Her book includes 225 direct references to such commentators and 339 items listed for "further reading."

Weiss reports, to begin with, that most of the discussions of social science research utilization have been normative, not analytical and empirical. They have proceeded on the explicit or implicit normative assumption that more use of the social science research in policy-making and decision-making is a good thing, ignoring the possibility that use of such research might by dysfunctional either for some groups in the society or even for the society as a whole. That is not to say that, with all proper caution as to objectivity, investigation of the relations between social research and social policy cannot make normative recommendations on the basis of an analytical and empirical approach. But such an approach is the essential prerequisite for normative prescription. That is the position I hope to adopt successfully in this book: I think that the use of social science for policy-making is on the whole, when the balance of its functions and dysfunctions is taken, a good thing. I hope to achieve, even given this normative predisposition, analytically relevant and empirically valid hypotheses and patterns about social research and social policy.

Weiss also discusses, in her survey of previous work, what she calls "the current enigma," the "paradox" that "observers in government and out find few instances in which research conclusions visibly affect the course of policy" (p. 3), even though the federal and state governments spend large sums in support of social science research and proclaim their intention to use this research. (In the chapter on James Coleman's research on youth and high schools, we shall see that his first research on the effects of segregation in schools was actually mandated by congressional legislation, but it was finally not used by either the legislative or executive branch of the government as a basis for social policy. It had effects on social policy only through the judicial system.)

Weiss explains the paradox as due in part to two mistaken assumptions that many social science researchers have about government use of their work. First, social researchers define as "use" only "the direct and immediate application of the results of a social science research study to a particular decision" (p. 10). As Weiss's own study shows, this mode of use is infrequent; there are many other and indirect uses of social science research. (This finding is supported in the eight cases reported in this book.) In one synoptic statement Weiss says:

> Social science research can affect the premises of policy argument. It can provide concepts, sensitivities, models, paradigms, theories. Such conceptual derivatives from research can influence which issues are placed on the policy agenda and which kinds of policy options are considered. They can enter into decision makers' orientation toward priorities, the manner in which they formulate problems, the range of solutions they canvas, the criteria of choice they apply. Since the processes by which decision makers absorb understandings of this sort are subtle and indirect, they may not be able to identify specific social science studies that influenced these—nor are observers likely to recognize them. [p. 12]

Second, social science researchers believe that social science, almost by itself, has the power to "make society happy, healthy, and wise" and that it will "inevitably benefit society" (pp. 13, 14). But the workings of society and social policy are not so benevolent or simple as this assumption has it. Political forces, partisan interests, and a variety of social structural and cultural constraints often limit the applicability and effectiveness of social science research.

Going further in her synthesis of previous discussions of the effectiveness of social science research for policy-making and including her own research findings, Weiss classifies three general types of "obstacles to research use." The first is that the research-producing system may itself be deficient, by producing studies that are poor or irrelevant for the policy and decision problems at hand. From the existing discussions of faults in the research-producing system, Weiss culls no fewer than seventeen specific ways in which research can be poor or irrelevant or both. The second general type of obstacle occurs in the decision-making system. The literature points to some ten specific ways in which decision-makers are unwilling or unable to use social science research. And finally, in the information-transmission system, she finds that the existing literature shows some eight different specific kinds of obstacles to the use of social science research.

Clearly, there exists in the specification of these thirty-five "obstacles" a considerable knowledge about the relations between social science research and social policy. But it is not systematic, disciplined, always empirically based knowledge. Weiss describes the existing literature as being "speculative," consisting of "insights," merely "illustrated" by personal experience, and not supported by carefully comparative research (p. 23). The important question remains, therefore, of which insights and illustrations and generalizations are correct. Which obstacles are constant and which occasional? "No investigations," says Weiss, "have systematically examined [the obstacles'] comparative effects" (p. 23).

Weiss's own study is designed to present just such a systematic and comparative examination of the insights that can be found scattered in a large literature. And that is what I also will try to do in this book, to compare the experiences of eight social scientists whose research has been in some measure effective in policy by asking them all the same questions, to be described below. By comparing the responses of these social scientists to a uniform set of questions, I hope to discover patterns that will be based in the actual empirical cases these social scientists represent.

In addition to its synthesis of the previous literature, Weiss's study provides a second valuable reference point for my book. By its particular method and scope, Weiss's book helps to highlight the purposes and limitations of my own work. Her carefully designed survey of the decision-making process among middle-level executives in the mental health field in federal and state agencies uncovers in a new and provocative way the exceedingly complex nature of the process and especially the indirect, "background" fashion in which social science research is used, when it is used at all. By exploding the assumption of direct and immediate use she has made an important contribution to our understanding.

In contrast, the cases and patterns of use presented here cover influentials and decision-makers at many levels of the governmental and corporate structures, all the way up to the topmost positions in those structures. These cases cover eight different substantive policy and issue areas, from privacy to tax policy to governmental deregulation of the transportation industry. Moreover, they illustrate the effectiveness of social research not only in executive agencies but in legislative bodies, such as Congress, and in the judicial system and its courts as well. Weiss, of course, is very much aware of, indeed stresses as a virtue, the specificity and limits of her study. As she says, "Our inquiry thus concentrates on the middle phases of the research utilization process. . . . The earlier and later phases are both critical phases of the research utilization process. We do not deal with them in this study: we leave it to other research to study their operation" (p. 50). The cases presented here do cover all three phases and, like Weiss's study, they do so with specific empirical data. These data are, of course, just a beginning. I hope they will be followed by more data from studies using larger and more representative samples of social science effectiveness for social policy.

Theoretical Background and Intellectual Stimuli

My interest in the effectiveness problem derives from a variety of general and specific theoretical concerns in sociology generally and in the sociology of science in particular. Of the general sources of interest discussed at the beginning of this chapter, certainly both the purely cognitive/intellectual interest and the value/ideological concern are at work in this book. My intellectual interest in the sociology of science goes back to undergraduate days and my "chance" but fortunate contact at that time with teachers like P. A. Sorokin, Robert K. Merton, George Sarton, Arthur M. Schlesinger, Sr., and L. J. Henderson. The first intensive expression of my commitment to the sociology of science was contained in *Science and the Social Order* (1952), which attempted to provide a theoretical synthesis of what was known up to that time in the sociology of science, though that was not in any way an established sociological subspecialty then. The sociology of science has remained a continuing theoretical and research commitment to the present; this book is only the latest evidence of that commitment.[7]

It would not be hard to discern in *Science and the Social Order* both my cognitive interest and a strong value/ideological concern. Not only are science and rationality identified as central values in our society, but also my own faith in these values is affirmed. In other work, I have tried to combine objective analysis and value commitments of other kinds: to such values as equality, equity, and efficiency. I have endeavored to show how social science analysis and research can effectively advance these values all the while being good social science.[8] The theoretical background, intellectual stimuli, and value commitments I have described briefly in this section all underlie this present book.

Immediate Background and Methodology

In 1973, with John Lally, Julia Laughlin Makarushka, and Daniel Sullivan, I published *Research on Human Subjects: Problems of Social Control in*

---

[7] See also Bernard Barber and Walter Hirsch, eds., *The Sociology of Science* (New York: Free Press of Glencoe, 1962); Bernard Barber, *Drugs and Society* (New York: Russell Sage Foundation, 1967); Bernard Barber et al., *Research on Human Subjects* (New York: Russell Sage Foundation, 1973); Bernard Barber, *Informed Consent in Medical Therapy and Research* (New Brunswick, NJ: Rutgers University Press, 1980).

[8] See *Social Stratification* (New York: Harcourt, Brace, 1957) and *The Logic and Limits of Trust* (New Brunswick, NJ: Rutgers University Press, 1983).

Medical Experimentation.[9] That book reported the findings of two large empirical research studies, which we had carried out from 1969 to 1972, one of a sample of about 300 biomedical research institutions using human subjects and another of some 350 medical researchers who used human subjects. Evidence that we were even then concerned for policy issues is contained in our last chapter, "The Social Responsibilities of a Powerful Profession: Some Suggestions for Policy Change and Reform." Shortly after the publication of our book, and continuing for a couple of years, I became involved in a variety of social policy activities. As a working sociologist of science, I realized that these very experiences of mine would provide a good case study of the relations between empirical social research and social policy. I kept, therefore, a very detailed record of materials bearing on my policy activities with a view not only to write up an intensive case study of my own experiences and insights but also to providing a model for other cases of effective social research. I hoped eventually to collect a set of such intensive case histories from a variety of social scientists. This book is the final result of my early hope.

Because of the differential prestige and vulnerability to ideological involvement among the social sciences, comparisons among the several social sciences seemed desirable, and I decided to look for suitable cases of effectiveness in economics, political science, and sociology. Furthermore, to make such comparisons possible, as well as to discern general patterns and problems, it was essential to try to have comparable data, which might be obtained by asking in each case history exactly the same set of questions. The questions, derived primarily but not entirely from the sociology of science and knowledge, are presented below together with brief rationales of why each question is relevant and important. Some further questions were discovered to be relevant and useful as I analyzed my own case and interviewed the social scientists involved in the seven other cases. For example, I had not originally thought to ask these social scientists whether they had ever started journals to make their own research and that of other social scientists more visible and available for social policy. When I learned that a couple of the researchers had done so, I added that question.

The general topics covered in the questions, each topic divided into several very specific subquestions, are social and intellectual sources of the researchers' general scholarly interests and specific research, funding and other types of support, key findings, specific effects on policy,

[9] New York: Russell Sage Foundation.

the various modes of influence used in achieving these effects, social and intellectual resistances from others to this research and its policy effectiveness, general lessons learned about social science effectiveness in policy, and further research and activity that might have policy relevance.

After writing a draft of my own case, referring both to my original list of questions and to the thick dossier of materials I had collected on my actual policy experiences, I set out to get my "sample." It was obvious to me from the beginning that this could not be a "representative" sample in any complete sense. How could it be, when no one knows what the universe of cases of effective social science is? I relied on my own experience with the social science literature, on my wide and diverse acquaintance with social scientists in several universities, and on interviews with especially knowledgeable colleagues in sociology, economics, and political science.

Another methodological decision was to look only for those "with the disease," so to speak—that is, those cases where it was clear that in some sense empirical research had indeed been policy-effective. The phrase "with the disease" is intended to imply a clinical model of seeking out revealing cases as a first step, since there existed no "epidemiological" data about the actual distribution of cases of effectiveness. In a large sample of cases, it might have been possible to look for revealing cases of failure, of sought-for but missed effectiveness. These cases might have made for interesting comparisons with the actually effective cases. In the effective cases I did find, however, there turned out to be some compensation for the absence of entirely failed cases. Some of the social scientists representing effective cases had had experiences with or phases of ineffectiveness. Thus, internal comparisons were possible for effectiveness and failure.

A few valuable facts emerged in the course of my intensive search for effective cases. It quickly became apparent that even very knowledgeable social scientists find it hard to think of notable, highly visible cases where specific *empirical* social research had influenced social policy. They can, much more readily, think of cases where "big ideas," not based on specific empirical research, have presumably had some influence. Economists, for example, immediately mention Keynesian theory or, for more recent days, supply side theory. Political scientists mention Kissinger's or Brzezinski's big theories about global power politics. More slowly, after persistent probing, social scientists may come to mention relevant examples from either their own research or that of some close colleague or friend, none of these being very visible to the community at large of social scientists. After only a few inquiries, it became clear to me that there are very few cases of highly visible, widely acknowledged instances of the influence of empirical research on social policy. A classic example, James Coleman's research on school desegregation, is a striking exception. But most of the cases of effectiveness are what I came to call "quiet cases," out there, but not widely visible. Any eventual attempt to discover the universe of effective social sciences researches and to select a representative sample thereof will have to look for these "quiet cases." It would be very useful for the various social science professional organizations to collect these cases by suggesting their existence to their members and asking them to submit possible examples from their own or their colleagues' work.

How did I settle, finally, on the particular cases presented in this book? Sociology was relatively easy because of my more than forty years of experience and acquaintance. Like everyone else in the field, I knew of Coleman's case. Morris Janowitz, at the University of Chicago, I had admired for his work in many fields of sociology and knew very well in his research on military manpower problems and policy and its great influence. For a long time I had also followed Peter Rossi's continual involvement in applied social research; Rossi is one of the premier figures in that kind of work. In consultation with him, we finally chose only one of many quiet cases, his research on the effects of the payment of post-release unemployment insurance benefits on the recidivism of released criminals. Rossi's case is one that involves both failure and effectiveness.

In economics it was only after much inquiry that I was able to locate the three appropriate cases: Merton J. Peck on government deregulation of the transportation industry, Eli Ginzberg on manpower and human resources policy, and Joseph Pechman on comprehensive income tax policy. Ginzberg, a Columbia colleague, was a quiet case who did not occur to me immediately. I also knew political scientist and lawyer Alan Westin as a Columbia colleague active in research and policy in the area of privacy and other civil liberties. It was not only to me but to other Columbia social science colleagues whom I sought out for advice in collecting my sample that Ginzberg and Westin were quiet cases. Similarly, at Yale, when I inquired of a very distinguished economist there, he did not mention his colleague Peck. I found out about him from a social scientist in Washington.

There are at least two reasons for the existence of all these, and probably many more, quiet cases, even in knowledgeable professional circles. First, many cases are of relatively small effect; that is certainly true of my own case and of others that have since been mentioned to

me. Second, high and increasing levels of research specialization in social science, not only between the broad disciplines such as sociology,
economics, and political science, but among the multiple subspecialties
of each discipline, keep colleagues ignorant not only of each other's
work but also of even such social policy effectiveness as exists. It would
be useful if this book raised the level of consciousness among social
scientists about quietly effective empirical research.

In sum, while I knew that these eight cases could not be shown to be
representative, nonetheless I felt that they were likely to suggest some
of the major patterns of the modes of consequentiality of empirical social research for social policy. These patterns could be elicited by asking all respondents the *same set of questions;* from the answers the patterns would emerge. The case studies are indeed very specific; they are
not general, vague allegations of policy effects. In the last chapter I shall
describe the patterns that did appear in the cases.

Limitations of This Book

I have already indicated that one limitation of this book is that the cases
are not representative. Other limitations have been deliberately imposed. I want to emphasize strongly that these cases are *not* final,
definitive accounts of the events, issues, and actions they report. Such
accounts await, if they are ever considered interesting enough to war-
rant such attention, their impartial, industrious, thorough social histo-
rians. The present accounts are of considerable current interest and are
bound to be an essential ingredient of any final definitive histories.
They are specific oral histories, which can be checked, enlarged, supplemented, and corrected in any final account by other materials, wit-
nesses, partisans. One way of constructing more complete accounts
would be to provide more of the "contexts" of these cases—that is, the
social, cultural, political, economic, and even personal factors that have
not been reported here. While all of the cases presented here do include some contextual material, they do not claim to be complete.

Another imposed limitation of these cases is that they are not up to
date as of the date of publication of this book. My own case was written
in 1982, and the interviews on which the other cases are based were
conducted in 1983 and 1984. Nearly all of the cases involve matters of
continuing social and political policy concern, and it did not seem
practicable to me to bring them up to date. Readers interested in particular cases will probably be familiar with recent events in these policy
areas or will know where to get the necessary knowledge. For example,

Pechman's recent views on comprehensive income taxation, and specifically on the 1986 tax legislation which partially embodied his ideas can be found in his new book, *The Rich, the Poor, and the Taxes They Pay*.[10] And Alan Westin's latest research findings and policy recommendations on the subject of the effects of office automation on the worker will soon be forthcoming.

I want to make clear another deliberate limitation. I have limited myself here to seeking patterns of effectiveness on social policy of carefully specified empirical research *programs* (sometimes extending throughout the scholarly career) or of particular and more circumscribed *pieces* of empirical social research. This is certainly not the only way in which social science has had and will continue to have effects on social behavior, social problems, and social policy. For example, many social science concepts, terms, phrases, and basic ways of thinking, often not based on specific empirical social research, have changed the way public opinion and policy-makers see the world and act to stabilize or change it. A classic indication of this fact was President Nixon's remark at one point in his presidency when he was recommending a certain fiscal and tax policy, "We are all Keynesians now." Another phrase derived directly from social theory and not from empirical social research is Robert K. Merton's "self-fulfilling prophecy," a term now used by the President and the man-in-the-street alike, by social commentators and social policy-makers on all kinds of issues. It has become a standard part of the language. Almost no one, except a few members of the professional social science community itself, would think of putting it in quotation marks or attributing it to social science in general or to Merton in particular. Yet, the concept dates only from the 1940s, enunciated first by Merton in an essay of social commentary in a general intellectual magazine of the time, the *Antioch Review*. Other terms (for example, "role models") have had a considerable effect on the way in which the public and the policy-maker visualize and deal with the world. Such terms are another example of the quiet effectiveness of social science.

Working Procedure

Having constructed my initial list of questions from the sociology of science, used it to write up my own case as a prototype and suggestive

[10] Boulder: Westview Press, 1986.

model for others cases, and searched out the possible and suitable cases, I approached each selected social scientist, asking for cooperation and explaining my purpose and plan. Fortunately, the cooperation was always readily and even gladly given. Many of the researchers said they were happy to have the opportunity to reflect on their own experience as well as describe it; they all had a certain general interest in the problem of the effectiveness of social science research. Some of my researchers reported that they had already made informal statements in class lectures or thought of doing on their own something of the kind I was now offering them the opportunity for: to make a considered statement in terms of their experience and research. For their interview with me, some of them made special efforts to refresh their memories of earlier phases of their research careers and their participation in policy by consulting their records and their writings.

After scheduling and interview, the modal time for which turned out to be two hours, I sent the prospective interviewee a copy of the list of questions and a copy of the manuscript of my own case. I hoped thus to illustrate and thereby call forth the specificity of response I was seeking. The interviews were tape-recorded, transcribed, and then "coded" by me for the content before I wrote a first draft. The coding was necessary because the interviews were not as neat and orderly as my list of questions. My researcher-interviewees spoke quite freely and concretely about their experience; they did not, fortunately, feel rigidly bound by the set order of my list of more analytic questions. As they told their stories, they skipped about, from earlier to later questions and back; they often linked questions from different parts of the list in order to cope better with the rich concreteness of their experience. I wanted substance from them, and got it, rather than mere orderliness. That could be somewhat restored later, and be all the better for it, after coding and the writing of drafts. Even in the drafts, however, and in the final versions as edited by the researchers themselves, I subdued the orderliness of my list when it interfered seriously with the substance of the researcher's own account and its basic "story line" as implicitly or explicitly constructed by him.

In accordance with my prearranged agreement with all the interviewees, having written a first draft, I sent it to them for comment: for corrections, additions, deletions, whatever. Again, I got excellent cooperation. Some interviewees corrected the drafts on some technical points. Others wanted to amplify. Some, to my regret, out of their caution or modesty, asked me to delete some of what they had said about themselves and their work. And some wanted to delete remarks made in what they now came to think of as "private" interviews from what they realized were going to be "public" accounts. I accepted, as promised earlier, all requests for change. None of them was remotely substantial enough to reduce the essential value of the final accounts of the cases. They are vivid, specific, useful accounts of researchers' experience with and reflections on the effectiveness of empirical research for social policy. The cases are presented in the alphabetical order of the researchers' last names; my own, since it was a prototype and more self-consciously constructed than the others, I have placed in an appendix. It did not appear helpful to order the cases in any other way than I have, by discipline, or specialty, or by policy issue. Such ordering might have been possible with a much larger set of cases, but, with only seven, alphabetical order, which constitutes a kind of impartial randomness, seemed the wisest course to follow.

The Questions and Their Rationales

I conclude this introductory chapter with an account of the questions I actually asked and why I asked them, in the hope that this will be a useful guide in reading the several cases. There were nine subsets of questions. I present each subset in the order that I presented it to the interviewees and I give a brief statement of the rationale for including that subset in the overall list. The rationales were derived from a number of sources: mostly from the sociology of science and knowledge, but also from such other specialties as the sociology of communication and of social change and from my own experience in research and policy activity in the field of the ethics of research on human subjects.

Early Training

How and by whom were you professionally trained? What were your original professional aspirations: theory, applied research, or some mixture?

We know from research in the sociology of science that such early training and aspirations often set the course for the novice social scientist's own work through at least the initial phase of his or her career and sometimes for a considerable part of even the whole of the career. Previous research has tended to study how researchers choose and commit themselves to particular scientific specialties and research topics, that is, to particular kinds of substantive science. I wanted, because of my interest in the effectiveness problem, to see how early training and aspiration also determine commitment to either basic or applied research or some mixture thereof. I hypothesized that this kind of commitment might well be as much influenced by early training as substantive specialty and topic commitment. The degree of effectiveness of social science may, thus, be influenced by the way in which early training and aspiration mold the purposes of individual researchers.

Sources of Empirical Research Interests

What were the different and probably multiple sources and purposes of your research?

- Were they theoretical, that is, to develop or test a social science theory, small or large—for example, to develop and test a theory of the nature of the professions?
- Were they methodological, that is, to try out or develop some method for the collection or analysis of data—for example, to try out the usefulness of path analysis or to test the effectiveness of telephone interviews in survey research?
- Were you concerned with general value or more specific norm relevance, that is, to increase awareness of, increase concern for, or stimulate action in behalf of some value or norm—for example, to increase equality for women by uncovering patterns of discrimination against women?
- Did you have specific social policy goals, that is, to get a law passed or some administrative practices changed—for example, to improve social and physical facilities for the handicapped in general or the blind in particular?
- Did you start with one or more of these purposes and gradually develop concern for one or more of the others? What moved you to these other concerns?
- If you became a social activist on behalf of your purpose or goals, what were the effects of this activism on your intellectual activities and career?

The rationale for these questions is to ascertain the differential influence on the interviewee's research of a number of social and cultural elements that have been alleged, in the sociology of science and knowledge and in the philosophy of science, to determine the choice of problems and the subsequent findings of scientific work. These elements are particular theoretical commitments, special value or norm preferences, scientific methodology preferences, and the pursuit of particular policy goals. In the first volume of his magisterial biography, *John Maynard Keynes*,[11] Robert Skidelsky addresses the problem of the differential effects of these various elements when he says of Keynes, whom many think of as the quintessential theorist, that he was not influenced primarily by "ethics" (that is, values), nor by "intellectual interests" (that is, theory), but by "practical events and goals" (that is, policy activities and goals).

This subset of questions is based also on established knowledge of the existence and great importance of the division of labor in science-making. We can now see, contrary to certain simplistic and even perfectionist views of the unity of science, that such unity as exists is often achieved through a somewhat messy and disorderly division of labor, with different scientists making different and specialized contributions that combine to move science forward. By early training and disposition, scientists specialize in terms of their commitment to theory, values, method, or policy; this specialization eventually produces some provisional near-unity. One kind of commitment is not, of course, necessarily exclusively preferred by any given scientist; he or she may combine them or shift from one kind to another, depending on the research program or study. We know from studies in the sociology of science that researchers move from one topic to another as topics become "hotter" or more interesting intellectually to them or as topics become more or less fundable.[12] We know that they even occasionally move from one discipline to another. For example, some of the brilliant work in molecular biology forty years ago was done by a generation of researchers who started in physics or chemistry—for instance, such Nobel Prize winners as Salvador Luria and Linus Pauling.

I hypothesized in this subset of questions that my researchers might have changed their purposes, from theory to policy or vice versa, as their careers developed. They might combine these different elements in different ways over time, as new problems or findings emerged. Change and "chance" are frequent in scientific work. Not only expected findings but serendipitous ones can change a scientist's goals and purposes, with respect to not only substantive science but also the relative importance of pure and applied research. The image of the scientist or

[11] New York: Viking, 1986.
[12] Bernard Barber, "Fashion in science," *Mens en Maatschapij*, 43(1968), 501–14.

the inventor working endlessly on the same problem or technology is a partial view and romantic distortion that seeks to emphasize what does exist in science in great measure, namely, diligence and perseverance. But in fact there is also much imagination and flexibility in science, and these result in change and what is loosely called "chance" in scientific careers.

Finally, since scientists, like persons in other social roles, may suffer from role strain or role conflict, I asked my respondents whether they had taken on the role of social activist on behalf of some policy goal and whether such activism had affected their work or career. We know that scientists can combine these roles of successful scientist and activist under some conditions. What are those conditions? How do they cope with potential role strain? Cole and Zuckerman, in recent research, have shown how successful women scientists cope with the role strain of being busy scientist, wife, and mother all at the same time. The problem of being busy scientist and social activist presents an analogous challenge to research and analysis.

The Influence of Sponsors

From what different and possibly multiple sources did you receive funding and nonmonetary resources to carry on your research and policy activities? What were their different interests and purposes in supporting your research?

- federal, state, or local government
- foundations
- nonprofit voluntary associations
- trade associations, professional associations, or individual business firms
- private individuals

My third subset of questions addresses the problem of how outside "interests," which are alleged by one school in the sociology of science to be powerful in determining the direction and content of scientific research, affected the research of my respondents. These questions probe the nature and effect of monetary funding and of various nonmonetary resources. Not to have their research wrongly steered by funders and other "interests" is one of the things scientists mean when they speak about the freedom of research. Scientists would like to have support without strings. For this reason, among the diverse sources of support from American social research, most researchers prefer to get funds from those government agencies and foundations which attach few or no nonscientific conditions to their support. In practice, this tends to mean the National Science Foundation, the National Institutes of Health, and the major grant-giving philanthropic foundations, such as Ford and Guggenheim. Those sources of support with strong interest in particular outcomes of research or enjoining self-protective secrecy or restrictions on publication are deemed less desirable. Business corporations are considered by many scientists to be, *in principle,* undesirable funding sources. Most recently, this view has been expressed in the turmoil in the universities over the funding by corporations of research in molecular biology and biotechnology; but such university scientific protest happened earlier with regard to chemical and physical research and technology. In practice, both in the past and in the present, business support has been accepted but usually with precise stipulations intended to protect the autonomy of the scientists from the "interests." By asking my social researchers questions about their funding sources, I wanted to begin the investigation of how these matters stand for social scientists more generally.

Especially in the social sciences, nonmonetary kinds of support as the right of access to research sites, events, and data; moral approval for the research; or expert advice and consultation from relevant knowledgeable parties are at once indispensable and a potential infringement on autonomy from nonmonetary interests. Therefore, I inquired about these matters.

Main and Unexpected Findings

What were the key value-relevant and/or policy-relevant findings of your research, either of a single piece of research or of some long-term program of research?

- Were any of these unexpected; any definitely contrary to your preconceptions when you started your research?

The reason for these questions is quite simple. I obviously needed to know what these findings were before asking subsequently about their effects. Here also I raised the question of unexpected findings and of findings contrary to the researchers' original scientific, value, or policy preconceptions. Such unexpected and contrary findings can have considerable effect both on the substance of scientific development and on policy effectiveness.

Effectiveness

What small or large, direct or indirect effects on policy did your research have? Be as specific and concrete as possible. For example, your research:

- raised governmental or public consciousness (concerned awareness) about policy questions
- contributed to getting a federal, state, or local law passed or changed
- contributed to getting a special interest group established to work for the policy your findings recommended
- contributed to changing the policy of some organization in the private or nonprofit sectors.

The basic rationale for these questions is the desire to avoid loose and vague statements, a common shortcoming in discussions of social science effectiveness, as Weiss's survey and synthesis found. My injunction to the researchers was "be as specific and concrete as possible" in order to avoid such looseness. In addition, knowing that social and cultural change in all fields, and not least of all in science and technology, proceeds often through many cumulative small steps, I inquired of my researchers about the small as well as the larger policy effects of their work. I also inquired after indirect effects. (One of the findings of Weiss's own study of decision-making among middle-level mental health agency executives is that a great many of the social science research influences on them are indirect.)

We know from the study of social problems that such problems as "poverty" or "sexism" often do not "exist" until public and then governmental consciousness of the problem is created by certain writers, the media (sometimes through "scandals" they portray), and protest movements. Public consciousness about a social problem is a necessary if not inevitable prelude to policy action and possible research effectiveness. Thus, in looking for possible effects of my respondents' research, I asked first of all if their research had indeed created public or governmental consciousness of a problem. Then I asked about other kinds of effects—on legislation, on special interest groups, and on organizations in the private and nonprofit sectors. Such effects are also determinative of social policy, whether to stabilize or to change it.

Modes of Influence

What were the multiple modes through which your research and policy activities exerted some influence? For example:

- Your research was purposefully distributed to a group of political and professional special-interest influentials.
- You testified about your research before Congress or other governmental committees and commissions.
- You briefed administrative decision-makers and advocacy groups.
- You communicated with special-interest groups or the public at large through newspaper and magazine interviews, TV and radio appearances, special interest group meetings and professional group conferences, and general or professional book reviews.
- You counseled others who were writing or acting with regard to your policy topics.
- You trained students or gave them advice on further research on your policy topics.
- You found yourself becoming an information center and intermediary among researchers and activitists on your policy topics.
- You started a publication to advance your research-based ideas and policy recommendations.

Previous discussion of how social research has policy effectiveness shows that there are many ways in which such effectiveness occurred. Based on the literature and my own experience, I asked about the multiple modes of influence that occurred in the respondent's case. In any particular case, these modes often occur not singly but in combination, and I inquired about that.

A few words about each of these modes of influence.

Dissemination of Report.   Especially when the research is designed, either by the researcher or by the supporting sponsor, to have specific policy effectiveness, but even when this possibility occurs to the researcher only after the research is completed, a report of the findings of the research can be carefully distributed to key opinion-makers and decision-makers. Whether these deliberately distributed reports are read and acted upon and by whom, we do not know. Still, the practice persists in the hope that it may increase effectiveness. From Weiss's study we do know that decision-makers are influenced at least indirectly by what they read, but whether they pay special attention to what is sent to them by researchers we do not know. Here is a subject for more research.

Testimony. In the American political system, much influence on eventual legislation is wielded by the numerous standing and special committees of Congress and by the various *ad hoc* commissions that investigate and report on particular and urgent policy problems. Social scientists may even be members of such commissions or serve as staff when they concern social problems such as pornography, TV violence, racial conflict, or earthquake disasters, to mention a few examples. It is now common for social scientists to be asked or to volunteer to appear to give research-based testimony, and so I asked about such experiences and their possible influence.

Sometimes, also, social scientists are asked or volunteer to brief decision-makers or legislators and advocacy groups directly. I asked questions on this score and found that it had been important in several cases.

Use of Various Media. We know from the relevant research that one of the "laws" of communication science is that if a communicator wishes to have a message effectively received and acted upon, he should send it out many times and through as many different channels of communication as possible. In inquiring about policy effectiveness, therefore, I asked about all the different ways in which a researcher's findings and policy recommendations might get through to the attentive public and to legislators and decision-makers. I asked about TV and radio appearances, about newspaper and magazine stories, articles, and interviews, about book reviews, and about presentations at professional conferences and meetings. All of these channels of communication may be used, usually in combination, by some social researchers who are seeking to raise public consciousness about social problems and to influence policy on those issues.

Networks. Another kind of influence that I knew about not only from general sociological research but from my own experience is the influence that is possible from being a member of a research or policy network. Researchers are not isolated but are members of more or less formally structured "invisible colleges."[13] Fellow members of these networks or groups often come to a leading researcher seeking counsel and help about scientific and policy matters. When I asked about activities of this kind, I found they were numerous and far-reaching in my cases. Some researchers act as information centers for networks of colleagues sharing their research and policy interests. This role of intermediary can be an important source of policy effectiveness.

Academic Training.   Influence, especially for researchers located in universities and research institutes, is often wielded indirectly, through training graduate students and post-doctoral fellows in their special scientific and policy orientations and activities.

Advocacy.   Finally, in their wish to communicate findings, to enlarge the amount of research on their policy issue, or to influence policy by public advocacy, researchers may start a special professional or general interest publication. Since this mode of influence is not common and has not been studied heretofore, I did not initially ask questions about it. But when I discovered that two of my researchers had used this mode of influence, I asked about it of all my subsequent cases.

Resistance

Were there any sources of resistance to your research findings and policy recommendations? For example:

- value sources—that is, groups or individuals with different values or norms from yours
- intellectual sources—that is, groups or individuals with different theoretical or methodological assumptions from yours
- interest sources—that is, groups or individuals with special interest in their own finances, power, or prestige

Societies are complex webs or processes of interacting knowledge, interests, and values. These different elements may be somewhat in opposition to one another and therefore need to be accommodated to one another either by compromise, as happens frequently, or by the triumph of one over the other. Sometimes the accommodation is peaceful; sometimes there is conflict. In short, for each piece of knowledge,

[13] Derek J. Price, *Little Science, Big Science* (New York: Columbia University Press, 1963).

each interest, each value, there may be some "resistance" by other ideas, interests, or values.[14] Therefore, I asked about the various possible sources of "resistance" my researchers had experienced to their ideas and policy goals. Change in science, or in society more generally, is often hard-won. Effective social science must expect to have to overcome "resistances" of various kinds, from ideas, values, or vested interests in prestige, power, or money. I inquired of my respondents about all these forms of resistance.

General Conditions of Policy Effectiveness

Have your research and policy activities taught you anything general about any of the following important social science effectiveness problems?

- the relation between social science knowledge and social policy
- the nature and processes of political power
- the processes of social change in society

Here I shifted from specific questions to more general ones. Because they were experienced and reflective social scientists, I asked if these researchers felt they had learned anything general about the conditions of policy effectiveness. I asked their general views on the relation between social research and social policy, on the processes of social and political power in American society which affect policy effectiveness, and about the processes and possibilities for social change. Such views would presumably affect their own policy activities. The views are no substitute for systematic analytic research on these interrelated matters, but may provide insights and supplements for the patterns that appeared in their more specific responses to my earlier questions.

Continuity

What further and continuing research and policy activities have all your earlier work and activities led you on to? The same topic? Related topics? Larger theoretical or methodological concerns?

---

[14] See Bernard Barber, "Resistance by scientists to scientific discovery," *Science,* 134 (1961):596–602.

Finally, because the sociology of science is interested in patterns of both consistency and discontinuity in scientists' work and careers, I asked my researchers whether their earlier work and activities had led on to later and current work and policy activity. To anticipate my later summary of findings, I discovered both integration and discontinuities in the work of the eight researchers.

Chapter Two

James Coleman

Educational Policy for Youth and High Schools

James Coleman, trained at Columbia University, founder of the Department of Social Relations at Johns Hopkins University, and longtime professor at the University of Chicago, is highly esteemed as a methodologist. He has recently been contributing to social theory and has been a prolific source of research on educational policy for youth and high schools in the United States. When social scientists are asked to name those of their fellows whose empirical social research has had clear effects on social policy, Coleman's name is usually at the head of their lists.

Interview: Fall 1983

I was trained in sociology at Columbia in the 1950s. My teachers were an extraordinary set of people. Three were most important: Paul Lazarsfeld, Robert Merton, and S. M. (Marty) Lipset, who was then an assistant professor. He had himself been trained at Columbia. I worked most closely with Marty on the ITU (International Typographical Union) study (*Union Democracy,* by Lipset, Martin Trow, and Coleman). Next most closely I worked with Lazarsfeld, especially on his work on panel studies and other methodological issues. I also worked with Bob Merton, but in a less intense way. For example, I took notes for him in one class, but I never worked directly for him on a project or otherwise.

Working so closely with these three men both formed and reflected my conception of myself as a sociologist. I didn't really see myself as a methodologist or a theorist but as something which encompassed both of these. I didn't see myself primarily doing applied research but I saw my work as including applied research. Anyone who worked with Paul Lazarsfeld got the conception that all sorts of things useful for fundamental knowledge could be gained from applied research. So I had a picture of what I wanted to do and be as someone making contributions both in methodology and in fundamental ideas within the discipline of sociology that could be labeled theory.

As it has turned out, I have done some of all these things: methodology, theory, and empirical research that has had policy consequences. It is the last of these that you have asked me about. During the past thirty years, I have engaged in a wide range of research on American youth and education. The first research I did is reported in *The Adolescent Society*. This focused on the social systems that exist among youth in high school. It didn't have any direct policy impact but may have had a long-term policy effect. Something related to the issues examined in *The Adolescent Society* was a report of a panel I formed when I was a member of the President's Science Advisory Committee (PSAC) in 1971–72. It was a panel on youth made up of people from various social sciences and educational practice and produced a report titled *Youth: Transition to Adulthood*. It was one of four reports on the structure of high schools that came out at about that time. It addressed the problem of whether the process through which schools bring youth into adulthood is appropriate. We raised a number of questions about the curriculum, about modifying it in ways that would include more possibilities for young persons to engage in nonclassroom activities before they graduated from high school. This report, again, did not have a direct effect on policy but did have an indirect effect.

The three main pieces of research that have had direct policy effects are the report published in 1966, *Equality of Educational Opportunity;* the report that I wrote for the Urban Institute on demographic effects of school desegregation, which was very much linked to the *Equality* study because they both focus on school desegregation; and the third, and most recent, is the *Public and Private School* book which is also seen by some as closely related to the desegregation issue.

Let me say a little more about each of these three studies. Although, with hindsight, they show continuity of interest, they have different origins that are of some interest; I had different reasons for going into each of them. I was approached in 1965 by Alex Mood to direct a research on equality of educational opportunity; and I agreed largely for disciplinary reasons. In the current context, it's hard to see things from the point of view of 1965. But it seemed to me, at that time, that social research was not having any serious, practical effect on government policy. Once in a while a few senior people were called in to advise, but that was the role of sociology as a policy science. I felt that, in the long run, for sociology to be justified it had to have some kind of payoff for society. It seemed to me that it was important for this work to be well done and for there to be things of the sort that we now call "policy research," although at that time the whole idea of such work was almost wholly absent. Of course, at the same time I had some degree of interest in the substance of the matter, both the educational substance and also the fact that the study was directed toward equality of educational opportunity. That was a very worthy cause; it conformed with my values. Still, my primary interest was as I have described it, disciplinary.

The second study had a different origin. In 1974 I was asked by Bill Gorham, the head of the Urban Institute, who was putting together a book on urban America for the Bicentennial in 1976, to be one of a set of people who were writing chapters for that book on different aspects of urban America. Mine was supposed to be on education. We were asked to focus on what had happened in the past ten years. I decided to focus on several topics in education: authority issues, that is, problems of discipline and order and disorder in schools; problems of financing education; problems of achievement; and problems of school desegregation. This last topic was a major urban question at that time. It happened that the Civil Rights Commission had collected extremely good data on that matter since 1968. It had data on school-by-school racial composition. So I started out to show changes in school desegregation over the period 1968–73.

The third study, *High School Achievement: Public, Private, and Catholic Schools,* was done at the National Opinion Research Center. I was interested in the larger project of which it was a part for one principal reason. I had a strong feeling about developing policy research in a new way, on a different model than had been used before. I felt there should be some degree of participation by interest groups and interested parties in the very design of the study. So, in the NORC proposal to the National Center for Education Statistics for this study (which was to be done in 1980), we asked for support for a period of time to interview parties who had testified before Congress and before state legislatures about their issues of concern. We wanted the research to address those issues and to provide information that was important for the interested parties. I also very much wanted this information to be directly accessible to the parties at interest; I hoped that they could dial a telephone number and with a terminal get tabulations from the data. I wanted this no matter whether the party was the American Federation of Teachers, the National Education Association, the state of Texas, or whatever. Unfortunately, NCES did not agree to that part of our proposal.

Our proposal had listed ten possible topics to the National Center, of which they selected five. I asked four of my colleagues at the University of Chicago and NORC to choose among the five topics. One took discipline in the schools, another took work and education (that is, work during high school), a third took changes in achievement between 1972 and 1980 (there was already a study of 1972 high school seniors), and a fourth took Hispanics in American education. I took the one that was left, which was public and private schools; that's how I came to that study.

Looking back now on these three pieces of research, I can see that I came to be more and more explicitly concerned about policy research and its character. I became more and more interested in the proper role of information-gathering instruments in relation to government and society; I considered social policy research such an instrument. It became part of my macrotheoretical interests. Should publicly funded research be designed only for use by public agencies, or by private groups as well? Should it be a pluralistic process? In my work in social policy research I have come to have two roles, one as a policy researcher and the other as observer and theorist about the macrostructure of society.

Since many sociologists see me primarily as a methodologist, I should say a word about that. In each of these three research projects there was the possibility of using more methodologically innovative techniques. For example, I used multiple regression techniques of analysis in the first study even though it was not something I had been brought up with and my own methodological innovations were in quite different areas. Still, I used multiple regression techniques and came to be as knowledgeable about that as I could in a short period of time rather than attempting to make methodological innovations in the policy research itself. Thus, my methodological work has been segregated from my policy-related research. There was one exception, a minor one, to this general pattern. For the second of these studies I did develop a new index of segregation because I was not satisfied with the existing indices. This index was based on a kind of measure of contact between black and white students in a given school system; it has come to be fairly widely used since.

In stressing my policy research concerns and describing how I felt about methodological innovation in these studies, I don't want to leave out my concern for more general matters of the structure and values of the society. This concern went beyond the immediate policy concern of school desegregation. Starting with the first study, I was very much concerned with the general structure of our society and with one of its central values, equality. I was, of course, only expressing quite widespread concerns in these matters. The first study was done immediately after, and as a consequence of, the Civil Rights Act of 1964. It was a time when blacks still found it very hard to get the kinds of rights which we now take for granted. For example, I was then teaching at the Johns Hopkins University, which was in the state of Maryland. And Maryland had a trespass law which allowed anyone who operated a business open to the general public, such as a restaurant or a bar or an amusement park, to prevent anyone they wished from coming into that place. The law was used in all these kinds of places to prevent blacks from coming in. There were a number of demonstrations against this law and this practice. In fact, my whole family and I were thrown into jail one night for participating in one of these demonstrations in an amusement park in the city of Baltimore. It was a time when people felt strongly about civil rights and equality, a time when those rights did not exist for the blacks. Although it was ten years after the *Brown* v. *Board of Education* decision by the Supreme Court, nearly all of the Deep South was still segregated. Only the border states had desegregated their schools. One of the striking things I found in the 1975 study was that in one year, in 1970, the statistics on racial composition in schools showed that the Southeast changed from the most segregated school region of the country to the least segregated. In the sixties, all of the injustices of segregation and inequality were still very much apparent to everybody; certainly they were to me. I thought, as I still do, that the issue of equal rights was a very important issue for America to address at that time.

The resources and support I needed and got for carrying out my three studies were of quite different kinds. The *Equality* study was a direct result of a provision of the Civil Rights Acts of 1964, Section 402, which required that the U.S. Commissioner of Education make a survey of the lack of equality of educational opportunity by race and other characteristics. I was released from half of my teaching at Johns Hopkins, where I was at the time, and worked simultaneously as a consultant and as the director of the project (with Ernest Campbell as co-director) in the National Center for Educational Statistics, which was the responsible agency of the Office of Education for this project. Since a requirement of Section 402 was that a report on the state educational opportunity be presented to the Congress on July 4, 1966, we prepared the report for that date. This may have been the first case in which a specific social research project was explicitly requested in an act of Congress.

The second study, for the Urban Institute, was done on a shoestring, with internal institute funds. The Urban Institute is a nonprofit organization which gets most of its funds from grants and contracts from government agencies, with additional funds from nongovernmental sources such as foundations and special interest organizations. The money for my research came from their "free funds." My study grew out of a chapter in Bill Gorham and Nathan Glazer's book on urban America, but became a separate report. I had moved to the University of Chicago by that time and did the work at long distance, so to speak. I had a research assistant located at the Urban Institute in Washington and would go there once in a while, as necessary. My programmer was also located there. He did the runs on the data and the research assistant did a lot of other things and among the three of us we were able to do the study on a shoestring.

The third study was again supported by the National Center for Educational Statistics. In 1972 they had done a national survey on high school seniors and they wanted to repeat it in 1980. This time they wanted to include sophomores as well as seniors in about a thousand high schools, sampled to represent the U.S. population of sophomores and seniors. They sent out a "request for proposal" and Ken Prewitt, then the director of the National Opinion Research Center at the University of Chicago, now the president of the Social Science Research Council, asked me if I would participate and prepare a proposal for this competition. I saw an opportunity to pursue the concerns with "pluralistic policy research" that I described earlier. So we made a proposal, our proposal was chosen, and the NORC survey provided the data base for our report on public and private schools.

I should say something about the relation between the university and the research in each of these three studies. For the first study, Johns Hopkins very much encouraged me to do it and arranged for my necessary release time. They didn't give me any special resources, but then I didn't need them for that study. The work for the Urban Institute only marginally involved the University of Chicago, since it was done at the Urban Institute and with no special arrangements for my time. As for the third piece of work, that was entirely different. I could never have done that study without the University of Chicago and NORC. Even though I was the principal investigator, the regular staff of NORC was necessary to the research, in design of the research, in management of the project, in sampling, in constructing the questionnaire, and in the field work. The intellectual, managerial, data collection, and clerical resources at NORC were extremely important. It is clear that for some kinds of research, such as this research on high schools or the study of the effects of the negative income tax, or other major policy-related research like that, a research organization like NORC is necessary. It has capabilities that are necessary to supplement those of academics like me. For big social science of this kind, universities do not have the appropriate infrastructure. A university-linked organization like NORC, which is dependent primarily on government grants and contracts, has the infrastructure and can call on the intellectual resources of the university.

A distinction needs to be made between two things: one is data collection, which is very expensive, especially for large data files, and the other is data analysis, which is not very expensive. In my first and third studies, both the data collection and the data analysis were paid for by the government. In the second one, the data collection had already been done by a government agency and so the cost for data analysis was minimal. We had only to do computer runs on data which were already in existence. Of course, in all such studies an important resource that is furnished by the university are the graduate students and research assistants. In the first case, several of my graduate students from Hopkins came over to NCES with me and worked on various parts of the study under my supervision. Two of these students not only did dissertations based on this work but subsequently went on to specialize in research on education. This was surely a consequence of their participation in the project. While they were working with me at the National Center, they were working for the Office of Education and were still registered as graduate students at Hopkins. This was unusual, but worked well in that case.

As for the most recent ("High School and Beyond") study, again I had three graduate students who worked very intensively with me in doing interviews with the interested parties, which we included in our pluralistic policy research design. They helped me modify the design on the basis of these interviews and also helped write the report of the final research design. Then the three of them continued on the project, two of them working as part of the field staff, and one writing up some of the analytical reports. Finally, two other graduate students, Sally Kilgore and Tom Hoffer, collaborated with me in the public and private school analysis. They are co-authors with me both of the report to the National Center and of the book coming out of that report. Kilgore now has a Ph.D. and is teaching at Emory University; Hoffer is currently finishing his degree, in continuing work with the same data set.

One interesting question often discussed is whether the kind of research organization that is an essential resource for this kind of policy-related social science should be affiliated with a university. The fact that the National Opinion Research Center is affiliated with the University of Chicago means that there is a constant and necessary supply of good graduate students who are essential for this kind of research. Both at Johns Hopkins and at Chicago there have been very able graduate students available for such research. It's hard to work with permanent research assistants. The graduate students are eager; it's hard to do research without new blood, new ideas, from fresh cohorts of graduate students. They feel it's a great opportunity to be working on a potentially important project. They probably work as hard as they're ever going to work again. Combined with the necessary funding, these graduate students are essential resources for the kind of empirical social research I've been talking about.

Having described the background of this policy research, I will give a brief and perhaps over-simple description of their main policy-relevant findings before going on to say something about the ways in which they actually had some effects on social policy. In the first study, one of our findings was almost a methodological one, a result of the way we posed the problem. Ordinarily, quality of schools had been defined in terms of inputs to the schools. We asked about outputs, using achievement outputs as criteria for judging the relative quality of schools. Even though that was not exactly a result, I think it had an important effect in reshaping the way in which educational research questions were asked after EEOC.

There were two important results of this study. The first was that variations in family resources had a much greater impact on student achievement than variations in school resources. This finding shifted the balance in assumptions about where important effects on education were. The second finding—and of course this was important for understanding problems of school desegregation—was that, of all the different resources a board of education had any control over, the most important effects on a student's achievement were the background of *other* students, the fellow students. The population in the school was an important educational resource; it had an effect on the student's achievement apart from his own family background. That is directly relevant to school desegregation.

The results of the second study were simpler and more straightforward. Our data showed that the degree of segregation *within* the school districts had declined more sharply than total segregation, which includes segregation *between* school districts. The between-school segregation had stayed constant or, in some parts of the country, it had slightly increased. This raised for me the question, since all of the existing social policy was focused on desegregation within school districts, whether this within-school desegregation had not had effects on increasing the segregation between districts. This finding in the research led me to look at the question of what was the effect of desegregation on loss of whites in central city school districts. Many nonsociologists had raised this question of what has come to be known as "white flight." Looking at the data more closely, after this question occurred to me, we found that in the large cities—the twenty largest cities of the United States especially and to a lesser extent in the next largest forty cities—when school desegregation had occurred there was a very extensive degree of loss of white students from those cities. The students went primarily to the suburbs. This white flight seemed to occur only in large or medium-sized cities, not when desegregation occurred in towns or small cities. It was very much a function of the degree of existence of white suburbs around the central city. It was the combination of the difference in racial composition between the central city and its suburbs and the occurrence of desegregation in the central city that led to white flight.

In the third study, there were two important findings, one having to do with desegregation and the other concerning differential student achievement and its sources. Both the Catholic private schools and the other, non-Catholic private schools had many fewer blacks in them than the public schools, the Catholic schools having only half as many and the others fewer still. So it would appear that private schools increase the amount of racial segregation. However, *within* the private school sector, both Catholic and non-Catholic, the black students are more evenly distributed than in the public schools, so that decreases segregation. These two effects just about balance each other out. The existence of the private sector increases segregation because of the smaller number of blacks there but it decreases segregation because those blacks that are in the private sector are more integrated within the private sector than are the blacks in the public sector.

The other important finding is that, after careful analysis of various kinds, the evidence shows that certainly in the Catholic schools and probably also in the non-Catholic private schools there is definite, significantly greater achievement than in the public schools for comparable students. It amounts to about two grade levels in the Catholic schools and about one grade level in the other private schools. To give us more assurance that there really was more achievement in the private sector, we looked for its likely sources. We found that in the private sector there was a higher degree of discipline, of order in the school, and greater academic demands on the students. These two factors produce higher achievement for comparable students, whether it's within the public sector, that is, when you compare schools of different types within the public sector, or within the private sector.

Of course, in all three studies, some of the findings were not what I had expected; they were contrary to my assumptions. In the first study, for example, I expected we would find much greater resource differences between schools attended by blacks and those attended by whites than we actually found. If we had measured quality in the old way, by the explicit resources provided by the school boards, we would have found little inequality of educational opportunity; there was much more inequality in this measure between regions, between urban and rural schools, than between racial groups within a given region. That was a big surprise. The second big surprise was how small were the effects of the input differences that did exist. Whatever input measures you took that were usually used to measure quality of education (and some of them are crude measures—per pupil expenditures, teachers' education, number of books in the library, age of textbooks), they showed almost no effect on achievement. We did not in that study take measures of the kind that we did in the last study: the organization of the school, attendance, amount of homework, student class cutting, school dress rules, things like that. Those are the things our later research, as well as other studies, seem to show as having an effect on educational achievement.

In the second study, I was not expecting or looking for "white flight," but once I noticed the discrepancy between within-district segregation and between-district segregation I guessed it might be due to that. The data led me to the examination of "white flight."

As for the third study, when I try to reconstruct its history, I think of a general phenomenon that occurs in research. You begin, not knowing

what you will find, then find a result and then get enthusiastic about
that result, and pursue it further. It's not true that researchers are objective and unbiased. I had no prior conception of whether there would or
would not be higher achievement in the public or private schools. *But,*
once we began to find this result, of higher achievement in the private
schools, then I became less objective because of the fact that one has a
tendency to seek consistency. While I wasn't really surprised by the
finding that the private sector produces higher achievement, I wasn't really anticipating it. But what I was very much surprised at was that the
beneficial effect of Catholic schools (but not of non-Catholic private
schools) was much greater for blacks, Hispanics, and lower-class whites
than for higher-class whites. I would have expected it to be the other
way around, that the private sector would have its most positive effects
on students from a more educated background. But in the Catholic sector, the strongest effects are for students from lower backgrounds.

All three of these studies caused a good deal of public discussion,
but one thing I'm struck by is a secular change between 1966, when the
first results were published, and 1981, when the results of the last study
were published. That's a period of fifteen years. What has struck me is
that there's much attention paid now to social research results, both by
the media and apparently by the readers of the media. It seems to have
been a long, slow process, a long, slow buildup of public consciousness before there was a great deal of media attention to research results
on equal educational opportunity. Now the media attention is very
great—which leads to gross simplification of the issues.

As to the effects on government, I was surprised by the fact that in all
three of my studies, government groups and agencies seemed to take
little direct interest. Even though the first report, *Equality of Educational Opportunity,* was produced under government auspices, the federal government didn't seem to know what to make of it. The results of
the second study could have been very helpful if the federal government had wanted to get local school districts to desegregate, but since
that wasn't government policy at that time, the study wasn't used in that
way. But neither was the 1975 study used by any but a few of the local
districts to defend themselves against demands for massive desegregation. Similarly, with regard to the third study, no government body at
any level showed special interest, even though I did meet with the
Council of Chief State School Officers and talked to them at length
about the results.

The generalization that I've made as a result of this experience is
that since government bodies and agencies gain legitimacy from their

official position, they don't need the additional legitimacy of social research results unless there's a conflict between levels of government. When such conflict exists, then social research results are used for additional legitimation. But the parties that find social research results most useful are the ones that are in conflict with some governmental unit at federal, state, or local level. In my experience, the parties that have really used my research most are parties who are plaintiffs in court cases. Results of the 1966 study, and to a lesser extent those of the 1975 study, have been used in court cases and in congressional testimony, but not by the executive branch of any government. The results were used in several precedent-setting cases. The first of these landmark cases was presided over by Judge Skelley Wright in Washington, D.C., in 1968, the *Hobson* v. *Hansen* case. It was one of the first important school desegregation cases. The same study was used in the Keyes case in Denver. I testified in both the Washington and Denver cases. Then my results were used in a large number of other cases, for example, in Charlotte, North Carolina, which was the first of the busing cases, although I didn't testify there. So it's clear that most of the results in school desegregation came through the courts, and that's where the research results were used extensively. Certainly school desegregation has not come through Congress or through administrative regulations.

One of the reasons these research results became so widely known and used was that there already existed strong interest groups that became plaintiffs in court suits on behalf of desegregation. The Legal Defense Fund of the NAACP was the most prominent of these. For the third study, the relevant interest groups were those favoring private education, those seeking more government funds for the private schools, religious and nonreligious. The National Catholic Education Association asked me to give a presentation of my results a year or so ago at their annual meeting, but they haven't been active in pressing for legislation. They tend to keep a fairly low profile with respect to political lobbying. Apparently they feel if they press too hard they may be hurt in one way or another, get a backlash if they're too visible.

The channels through which my research results became known and had their influence were quite variable. In all three cases the sponsors of the research brought it to the attention of the press, the public, and various influential parties. In the first case, the Office of Education held a press conference on the date that the report was, according to the Civil Rights Act, required to be presented to the Congress and the President. But they were sufficiently concerned about any kind of political impact that both in the conference itself and in the design of the summary of the report they downplayed the results, essentially saying that the report didn't really show anything new. That was in part because they had just embarked on a policy of giving federal monies to the local school districts for buildings, and here was a report that showed that school buildings couldn't be shown to contribute to scholastic achievement.

For the second study, I gave a report of early results to the American Educational Research Association, an association composed of educational researchers. The *Washington Post* picked up the result that within-district school desegregation policies seemed to be increasing between-district segregation. That opened things up wide. It brought about a flood of people interested in the results. I had to hide away down on my farm to get away from reporters once that uproar had begun.

In the third case, the National Center for Educational Statistics, which had sponsored the study, did not let us release the report in a normal way. First they held it up for six months and then they created a media event in Washington, in a hotel ballroom and, to protect themselves, asked four critics of the report to speak. Fortunately, our results were consistent with those of Andrew Greeley, who had used some of the same data as I to examine the effect of public and private schools on minority students. This big media event was in April of 1981; two of the critics were academics, specialists in research in education, and the other two were engaged in educational policy and practice. I didn't like this media event; a number of academics felt that I was holding press conferences about my research, when the fact of the matter was that we had wanted to release the report in an ordinary and straightforward way six months before. One academic, an early colleague of mine, Robert Crain, who feels very, very strongly about desegregation issues, who has made his whole research career focus on that problem, actually distributed a critique of my report in the hall before the press conference began. He called up other academics and asked them to make public critiques. I think it was Crain's very strong ideological position that generated his strong stand.

A number of reporters wanted interviews following these various studies, and I did give some, though I have a general policy of not appearing on television, and I ordinarily discourage interviews. I find the mass media extraordinarily unsuited to the complexities of social research results. During the 1966 study I applied for a Guggenheim Fellowship, which I got, and escaped to England. After the second study, I did appear twice on television, which confirmed my belief that I should not do so.

Like other social scientists, of course, I've appeared a number of times before professional associations and meetings. Because of the conflict over my results, there have been plenary sessions arranged at which I and my critics were asked to present our cases. The most important of these was at the 1976 annual meetings of the American Sociological Association. It was arranged by the council of the association because of the discussion and conflict aroused in the association by the strong ideological opposition to me and my research by Professor Alfred McClung Lee, who was then the president of the association. I'll come back to this event later when I speak of various kinds of resistance to my research.

One of my activities which has had indirect influence on policy has been training graduate students to become researchers in this field. The kind of intensive research I've done requires a lot of work and commitment from graduate students; they get very involved. Several of my students have worked with me over a period of time, gotten involved, and then have been occupied with this area of research over the rest of their careers. For example, Jim McPartland, whom I asked, when he was a graduate student in 1966, to work with me on the study, has continued in much the same area. Education has been his career ever since, with a concentration on school desegregation. This continuity has been unusual, but since education and the desegregation issue have been a continuing issue over these years, it could become all of one's career.

I've already mentioned resistance to my work. Let me come back to that. I will speak first of the resistance, on theoretical and methodological grounds, although much of the value and ideologically based resistance was channeled through or intertwined with the theoretical and methodological criticism.

One fact that has interested me was that a lot of the initial methodological critique of the first study came from three pairs of economists. This was one of the first times that both economists and sociologists were working directly on the same institutional area. Moreover, this was one of the first times that economists had begun to try to examine educational activities which they described as "production functions" in education. So some of them were looking for equations and regression analyses which could show them the elasticities in this area: if you increase per pupil expenditure by 10 percent, then by what percent do you increase the student achievement, or by what percent do you increase the college-going? That was the way they thought. Thus, they had what I think turns out to be a fairly simplified view of the educational system. They were looking at it as if it were an industrial enterprise and analyzing it as if it were such an enterprise (though they might well find similar divergence from their theories if they were empirically serious about production functions in some industries). The fact that we didn't find the kinds of results that lent themselves to this kind of analysis led three pairs of economists to criticize the report on intellectual grounds, although probably in at least one of the cases value grounds were mixed in. The intellectual/ideological criticism came from the economists Henry Levin and Sam Bowles. Another critical paper was written by Eric Hanashek and John Kain. Another came from Glen Cain and Harold Watts at Wisconsin. All of these critiques were methodological ones, economics versus sociology. As with my students, some of these critics have stayed with this field.

Economists also, as a result of their views on production functions, have a different orientation toward policy research than I do. In the paper by Cain and Watts, they viewed regression coefficients as parameters to tell you precisely how much achievement output you will get per dollar input. They seemed to feel that with this kind of analysis they can tell the policy people, the administrators, just what policies to carry out. My view, of course, is that this is much too simple and direct an orientation. What is a more valuable result of policy research is the demonstration, to the administrators or anyone else interested in affecting policy in the field, of how they need to change their conception of how the system works. The role of social research is not to tell these people what policy to carry out. It should provide only one input to that process, to aid an understanding of how the system works, which might lead them to carry out policies they would not have tried before. I think we should promise much less direct effects on policy-making.

There were also intellectual differences, of course, with my colleagues among sociologists. With regard to both the second and the third studies, I was disputed on methodological grounds; I was criticized for some of the measures I used. For example, Karl Taeuber felt I should have used a different index of segregation from the one we used. He preferred another one with which he had long worked. As it finally turned out, no different conclusions result, no matter which index is used. The methodological dispute over indices of segregation arose especially with regard to the second study. Remember that this study was done for the Urban Institute, which had as a member of its board a person who was also an NAACP official. This person (who subsequently resigned from the board) didn't like my findings about desegregation and white flight; nor did the others. Bill Gorham, partly to reassure his board members and partly to reassure himself, convened a conference to discuss the methodology of my study, which included Karl Taeuber, as well as Thomas Pettigrew (who subsequently attacked me in print with some vehemence). Ideology and methodology came to be intertwined. Finally, most of these methodological issues got ironed out and all but the most committed concluded that my analysis was correct.

Even when I felt that the methodological issues had some ideological source or intent, if they were serious I treated them seriously, and that was useful. One of the things I've come to feel is that there can be a lot of methodological development, and possibly even innovation, as a consequence of some of these debates on policy research results. They focus attention more intensively on certain fine points of methodology than is true in academic research. Often, in academic research, people don't care that much, no one's job is at stake, no one's ox is being gored as much by a certain set of research results. But it's really surprising how relatively methodologically unsophisticated people can come to be extraordinarily sophisticated when their interests are at stake. Values and interests are very important because they do concentrate the mind. Thus, despite a certain positivist conception to the contrary, ideology is not useless. It can have a very intensifying effect, which is positive. This is especially true because scholars who have value differences search for methodological grounds on which to justify their position.

Some people, to be sure, like the NAACP person on the Urban Institute board, just flatly disagree on value grounds about raising the question of possibly negative consequences of school desegregation policy.

With regard to the findings of the third study, again there was some direct value difference and resistance. I had an intense discussion with members of the Council of Chief State School Officers. After my afternoon talk, though I planned to leave, they induced me to stay over and continue our discussion. An issue that one of them raised, which I think is an important value issue, was the issue of cultural pluralism in the schools versus the necessity for value consensus in a nation. Even if you don't look at the public schools as an effective melting pot, you do want to have some value consensus in society. In the public schools, especially in the United States, one idea behind the common school has always been that it helps to generate a value consensus in the society. Every nation, I think, uses its schools somewhat in this way. And my questioner asked, if you have too much separatism in the schools, too many people going to private schools, each of which has its own either religious or ideological character, aren't you going to have, in the name of pluralism, a fragmented society? That was a direct value confrontation, and a legitimate one.

Linked to value differences, in some cases, were interest sources of differences with my findings. For example, Al Shanker, in his criticism of my work, is clearly motivated by the interests of his union, the American Federation of Teachers, in maintaining a very strong public school system where they have much more security and power than they do in the private schools. Shanker, in defense of his union's interests, uses legitimate value and methodological criticisms.

How shall I sum up some of the general things I've learned over these years and these studies about the relation between empirical social research, on the one hand, and things like social policy and social change, on the other? I can repeat a few of the things I've already said. Social research needs to establish some legitimacy for itself as one input to social policy. Remember, however, that in my case it was mostly outsiders, interested parties who were trying to challenge government policy, who made the greatest use of our research findings. In other cases, the government agencies or actors might be seeking to strengthen their legitimacy.

Another point I have come to feel strongly about is that while empirically based social science knowledge is important for policy, there are always other kinds of value and political concerns involved in social policy. Social science results should not be the determining element in policy, but only one of a variety of inputs into policy decisions. And it should be an input that aids the pluralism or democracy of the policy process. There tends to be an orientation on the part of disciplinary groups that they ought to govern any activities that they engage in; nobody else ought to have anything to say about it. This is true especially with respect to the kind of research they ought to engage in; look at the reaction of biological scientists to the idea that others should have some say in recombinant DNA research.

As for social power, I feel that everyone ought to have access to whatever results come from publicly funded research. There ought not to be a private and closed communication between the researcher and a government agency. Societies in the future will have major problems concerning how people can maintain their autonomy vis-à-vis a powerful nation-state. For that reason we need to institutionalize all sorts of devices to make it possible for pluralism of power to survive. One element of this power is information, and social science research is one source of information.

Finally, I have learned that social change doesn't happen very fast. And, to repeat, I've learned in my case that social change does not always come about through legislative or executive action but may well come about through the courts. Only the agency which is most distant from popular control—that is, the courts—can afford to carry out unpopular policies involving social change. It's debatable, of course, whether courts should have the power they exercised in the 1960s and 1970s.

As to the future of my own research and work, this past work has raised for me some ideas, I won't call them theories, about the functioning of society on a more macrostructural level. As our society gets more complex, what are its various structural options? Social science research is going to be an essential provider of information in answering such questions. Discussing these options in the light of social science knowledge raises a number of intellectual and value questions. I expect to be concerned with those in the future.

Manpower and Human Resources Policy

*For more than fifty years, Eli Ginzberg, of Columbia University's
Graduate School of Business, has been engaged in a program of
research and a career of policy advising on manpower and human resources. He was also early in the field with regard to a
concern about womanpower. He has brought to his lifetime research program not only his professional training as an economist but a broad social and political perspective. His influence has
been wide, on governments in the United States and abroad and
on business corporations. For him, human resources are the basic
element in any social and economic system.*

Interview: Fall 1983

Although I have always identified myself, and been identified by others,
as an economist, I have always had broader intellectual interests and
broader social and political perspectives. Of course, when I was starting
out in economics in the late twenties and early thirties, it was a much
smaller, less specialized, less quantitative discipline than it has since
become. But other factors contribute to my broad interests and background. There was, first, my family. My father was a scholar of Judaica, a
professor of international repute, one of the fifty world scholars from
all fields who received an honorary doctorate in 1936 at the Harvard

Tercentenary Celebration. Scholars from many different fields, people of academic distinction, visited frequently in our home. I picked up from them, and especially from my father, not only some of their culture, but also their passion for quality.

My broad interests were easy to nurture when I entered Columbia College in 1927. I had the run of the college after my freshman year and had a unique kind of education. I studied anthropology with Franz Boas and Ruth Benedict: I had Robert MacIver in sociology, Shotwell in political science, Woodbridge in philosophy, and Wesley Clair Mitchell and John Maurice Clark in economics. I spent my sophomore year at Heidelberg University: my father was on sabbatical. That year had a substantial effect on me. For one thing, it made me see that I was more interested in economics than in history, my first love, though I had no idea then of becoming an academic. The ghost of Max Weber was still walking around in Heidelberg. And there were greats on the faculty such as Alfred Weber, Emil Lederer, who taught me economics, Heinrich Rickert, with whom I took philosophy, and Karl Jaspers.

When I returned to Columbia, my last two years were like early graduate years. I was pretty much free to do what I wanted. In my senior year, I took a course in the history of economics with Professor Thomas C. Blaisdell, Jr., who later taught for many years at Berkeley. The Edwin R. Seligman Library, which had a unique collection of seventeenth and eighteenth century economic tracts, had just been bought by Columbia. In connection with Blaisdell's course and using the facilities of the Seligman collection, I became interested in Adam Smith. I continued with this interest in Smith when I went on to graduate work in economics at Columbia. I was dissatisfied with the current interpretations of Smith's work. Eventually, I wrote my doctoral dissertation on this subject and called it "The House of Adam Smith." And this dissertation was published as a book, as Columbia then required all dissertations to be. There were a few biographies of Smith but mine was the first book-length study in English of his work. I interpreted him as a liberal reformer who sought to change the existing mercantilistic system of exchange into the market system. It was a successful book: for several generations graduate students were required to read it.

I really stumbled into using Smith for a dissertation. I was uneasy about writing a dissertation that was solely history or theory. I still wasn't fixed on an academic career. Our family had a banker friend who had an early Ph.D. in economics from Columbia and I knew that I might be able, like him, to use my economics training on Wall Street. I also knew that economics might help to get me a job in the government. The history and theory of economics were not what I needed for Wall Street or the government.

The biggest influence on turning me from history and theory to analytic and empirical work in economics was Wesley Clair Mitchell. He felt that I was bright, but he didn't approve of my interest in history and theory. In his famous course on current types of economic theory he showed himself to be a skilled historian, but he didn't think that was a field for serious research.

In the late thirties—I started to teach in 1935—I assisted Mitchell in a seminar on psychology and economics. But we could not successfully translate from contemporary theories of psychology into economics. It turned out to be a no-win game. That gave Mitchell strong leverage to push me toward empirical research. I had earlier helped to prove myself to Mitchell by turning down a great opportunity to take a job, for which he recommended me, at the University of Wisconsin. Jobs were very scarce in 1934. But I told Mitchell that starting to teach would interfere with the research that I was doing at the time. In Mitchell's value scheme, if it were a choice between research and teaching, one should choose research. Mitchell was the leader of empirical research in economics. My father was once told by his friend Professor Harry Wolfson, the Harvard philosopher, that Mitchell had said to him (1936) that he was "fighting for my soul." That's the way Mitchell felt.

I got my first chance to do some empirical research as a result of being awarded the Cutting Travelling Fellowship from Columbia in 1933. My mentor in the college, Harry Carman, who later became its well-known dean, had advised me to apply for the fellowship despite the fact that preference was given to children of American-born parents, which mine were not. Strings were pulled and I not only got the fellowship but was allowed to use it for work in the United States rather than for travel in Europe. It was a post-doctoral fellowship year for me. I visited Washington on my travels, where I was tempted by a well-paying government job but refused. I spent the year studying the nature and functioning of large American corporations. My findings showed most large corporations to be anything but efficient. That was the beginning of my long-term interest in large organizations, which has just resulted in a new book, *Beyond Human Scale: The Large Corporation at Risk*. The core of this new book goes back to a conversation about large U.S. corporations that I had with Mr. Justice Brandeis way back in 1934!

Another formative influence that propelled me not only into empirical but also interdisciplinary research came from my cousin, Dr. Sol W. Ginsburg. He was a broad-gauged psychiatrist, concerned with social problems, who suggested we undertake interdisciplinary research on the unemployed, of whom there were large numbers in those Depression days. Mitchell was very supportive and helped me (1939) to get some early financial support from the Columbia University Council for Research in the Social Sciences. The funds of the council came from the Rockefeller Foundation, which at that time was supporting the development of empirical social science. My first grant from the council was for $7,500, and the following year I received another $4,000, a considerable sum in those days. We did a study of the long-term unemployed in New York; another on the coal miners in South Wales; and a third, with the help of a graduate student who had active experience in the labor movement, on the leadership of the American labor movement. We published three books on these topics.

In carrying out the study of the unemployed, our team began to think about the question of work in a larger context: what the lack of work does to people. We became particularly interested in the problem of occupational choice. The United States had not yet entered World War II, but we were drafting young men. We studied a thousand young men who had been drafted, served twelve months, and then were discharged, to assess what effects if any their service had had on their future occupational choice. We published an article, "The Occupational Adjustment of a Thousand Selectees," in the *American Sociological Review*.

At about this same time, I had as a student a young woman who was a graduate of Vassar. I remember going up to Vassar to talk to the president, Henry Noble McCracken, about the occupational choices and later activities of his graduates. I was dismayed that so many of them went to the Katherine Gibbs School to train to be secretaries. I told McCracken that I felt there was something wrong in the interface between his curriculum and the world of work. So very early on I was interested in this problem of women's work but, because of the war and the whole social situation, nothing much came of it at that time.

By the early 1940s, with these early research and writing activities behind me, the purposes and structure of my future program were becoming pretty firmly established. I had identified and committed myself to a number of theoretical, value, and policy purposes that were basic to all of my future work. I have never had any special interest in methodological issues.

On the theoretical side, I had become interested very early in trying to understand what I would call the behavioral underpinnings of economics. My views were quite different from the simplistic notions that economists postulate about so-called rational behavior. I was deeply skeptical about the intellectual foundations of modern economics. I felt that the theory of economics needed considerable modification to be applicable for effective social policy. To carry out this theoretical task, I knew that I had to make a long-term commitment in my research. That was another influence that Mitchell had on me. By indirection, Mitchell made it clear to me that one would have to engage in long-term and focused activity. It couldn't be a hit-and-run affair. Even though I preferred a bite-at-a-time approach, I realized the importance of continuity in my several researches and books on a central area of theoretical concern. Therefore, I have conceived of my work, and I think others have so conceived it, as being primarily devoted to the structuring of the field of human resources and manpower. I am sometimes called the doyen of that branch of knowledge. I think that it was my work that popularized the concept and the term "human resources." As late as 1954, at the celebration of the Columbia Bicentennial when I was conversing with one of the most literate of the downtown investment bankers, he indicated that he had no knowledge of what the term "human resources" meant.

On the theoretical side also, one of my purposes has always been to show that interdisciplinary research is necessary for the adequate understanding of human resources. Our team has always been interdisciplinary. My cousin, the psychiatrist, was a member of my team for about twenty years. We brought in John Herma, a Viennese-trained lay analyst, who was also a student of Piaget. Early in our work, Milton Friedman helped us in the statistical design for the study of the unemployed in New York. We had psychiatric social workers on the staff. At one point, I counted at least seven or eight distinguishable disciplines among the staff on the Conservation of Human Resources project. I was always more interested in trying to understand a complex social phenomenon and less concerned about advancing the methodology of economics or one of the other social sciences. I still retained, of course, a broad interest in what our research implied for economics.

In addition to my skepticism about the applicability of economic theory as a guide to policy, I always had a concern with the real world and was committed to a set of values that I wanted to achieve. I wanted to change the real world. A major influence in this direction came from my mother. In contrast to my father, a man of exquisite culture who wrote articles and books in eight languages, my mother was an activist, always concerned with changing things. I've sometimes said that, between the contrasting influence of my two parents, the odds were that I would become a hopeless schizophrenic, unable to do anything. But by luck I was able to manage an accommodation between my two parents, the scholar and the activist. My mother couldn't have cared less about books and ideas. She wanted to make this a better world and was constantly and powerfully involved in social reform activities of various kinds. That was a big factor in my orientation to the world and to my research.

My research has had, explicitly or implicitly, a whole series of value concerns. I have been for greater opportunity for all, more equity, less discrimination. For example, our group undertook pioneering work on the issue of black manpower, the way it was wasted and underutilized. The book we published in 1956, *The Negro Potential,* was the first major postwar, empirically based analysis of the waste of manpower in the United States resulting from the discriminatory treatment of blacks. Our data came in part from the military. The military was a great laboratory for our research and for understanding the underutilization of blacks and what it meant not only for their frustration but how it harmed our society at large. Even earlier, *The Uneducated* (1953), a book we did with the encouragement and support of President Eisenhower, had illustrated the deleterious effects of lack of education on both civilian and military performance as well as on the individuals who had been shortchanged.

There was another value, the efficiency/performance value, that was behind our research. As an economist, I placed a high value on work. Work is one of the most binding phenomena in all society. Access to work, opportunities to be productive in work, to be promoted on merit, to have decent rewards, all of these have been concerns to our research group for a long time.

I didn't rest content, in guiding our research efforts, just with general values. I tended always to have some concrete and specific policy reforms in view. For example, in our studies of the unemployed, from the very beginning we sought a better policy for dealing with people who had lost their jobs. During the project, I developed an easy relationship with the Welfare Department in New York City, which was administering the unemployment relief program at that time. Because I wanted to understand what unemployment did to people, how they responded to such a basic challenge to their way of life, I studied not only the unemployed themselves but their families. This forced us to look for better policies that might help preserve family structure and better protect the children of the unemployed. When Dr. William C. Menninger testified in favor of the new policy embodied in the Employment Act of 1946,

he cited our earlier study of the unemployed, particularly the effects of
unemployment on the family. We got to know each other in the Surgeon General's office during World War II where I had given him a
copy of the book in which our research was reported.

From the earliest days of World War II, I was very much involved
with manpower policy in Washington. Owen D. Young, the chairman
of the board of General Electric, was the head of a Committee on
Scientific and Specialty Personnel. As a member of the Technical Advisory Committee, I submitted a number of memoranda about the draft,
women, and other aspects of emerging manpower issues. Since we still
had 10 million unemployed in December 1941, the committee wasn't
particularly receptive to most of my policy recommendations aimed at
conserving manpower. I told them that all our unemployed would disappear very quickly as the military expanded and that we would need
all the college-educated women we could entice into jobs.

A little later, in the fall of 1942 when the war was in full swing, I
became the manpower adviser to General Brehon Somervell, the head
of the Army Service Forces. I had become acquainted with him when
he was the Works Program Administrator in New York when we were
engaged in studying the unemployed. The Army Service Forces at that
time was the largest work organization ever put together in the United
States, some 2 million people. I remained a civilian, even though attached to a military organization. When the chief of staff, General
George C. Marshall, told Somervell that he had to cut back, I was given
the job of constructing a policy for reducing the organization. We took
180,000 people off the payroll of the Army Service Forces in ninety
days. In addition, we transferred 60,000 people from the Army Service
Forces to the Ground Forces. I worked out a rationale for these manpower policies and wrote it up in a position paper entitled "Work Load
Studies for Personnel Strength Control." We stamped it with Somervell's
three stars and made it operative. Fortunately, the labor market was
able to absorb almost all the discharged people immediately. Because
the Army Service Forces had grown so fast and with so little control in
the early days of the war, the reduction was no great loss. Some people,
in the disorder, had even been getting two paychecks!

In the second part of the war, I became the logistical adviser to the
surgeon general of the army with oversight over all the manpower and
other resources under his control. The total manpower consisted of
about one sixth of the entire army. At peak we had about 60,000 ser-
vicemen in hospital beds at one time and another 700,000 were taking
care of them and the rest of the army. I prepared the design and the

detailed plans that established the specialized hospital system that the army put in place. My policy was to concentrate the relevant medical specialists in selected hospitals and to ensure that those who needed specialized medical attention were transferred to the appropriate location. It proved to be a very effective way to deliver a high level of care.

After the war, in early 1946, when General Bradley became the head of the Veterans Administration, I was asked by him and his chief medical officer, General Hawley, to stay on in Washington and design a VA system similar to the one I had constructed for the Army Medical Department. But I decided against that in favor of returning to Columbia. Still, because of my interest in policy, I was determined to keep one foot in Washington. And I did. From the fall of 1941 to 1982 I was continuously in some kind of advisory position in Washington. People sometimes speak of in-and-outers, that is, people who alternate between government and the university. I was a perpetual inner. I deliberately did not affiliate myself with either political party. I wanted to operate in the policy field as a British civil servant is supposed to, giving advice to whatever party is in power. I not only kept up my relations with the bureaucracy but managed, over the years, to have some kind of advisory role with each of the incumbent presidents.

Most important and unusual of all these connections was the one that developed with President Eisenhower. Through General Howard Snyder, Eisenhower's personal physician, with whom I had worked closely during the war, I was introduced to Eisenhower when he was chief of staff and president-designate of Columbia University. Eisenhower felt that the manpower lessons of the war should be studied and reported. He felt that unique records to undertake this important social research were available. And he wanted to know why 3 million young people had not "made it" in the military, either because they were unsuitable as recruits or because of failure as soldiers. When Eisenhower came to Columbia, he asked me to carry out these studies. We took my embryonic research group and turned it into a much enlarged organization that we called Conservation of Human Resources. That organization still exists and has been doing manpower studies ever since 1950.

All of these examples from the war and after indicate the way in which I was concerned in designing policy-relevant research focused on manpower problems of large organizations, first in the government and later in private industry. During the Korean war I became an active adviser again to the military. I enjoyed seeing at least some of my recommendations turned into organizational policy. Often I failed. For example, when I pressed Frank Pace, who was then the secretary of the army, to change some of the criteria and standards for military recruitment and training, he said he could not do it by himself. He arranged for me to talk with the chief of staff and the deputy chief, and the rest of his cabinet but they refused to alter their manpower policies.

All the purposes of my research program—theoretical, value, and policy—were always pretty much intertwined. Sometimes I gave more weight to one or the other facet, but I didn't think of them as separate. I took the different opportunities for work as they offered themselves, or as I could find them, to pursue my broad programmatic approach.

I have always been fortunate in getting funding and finding or creating the other resources required for our research. Of course, back in the late 1930s, we managed on very little funding. For example, in our study of the New York unemployed, neither my cousin, who was my collaborator, nor I, took any salary. We used the money we got from the Columbia Council for Research in the Social Sciences to hire a part-time secretary and some part-time psychiatric social worker interviewers. Even earlier, my Cutting Travelling Fellowship had paid my bare living expenses, little more.

Eventually, however, and especially after the Conservation of Human Resources was established, we obtained larger funds. Later on, because we had a long track record of substantial research and publication in the field, when the Department of Labor got new authority in 1962 to enter upon an external research program for manpower and human resources, we became an important contractor. In the twenty-year period from 1963 to 1982, we received about $250,000 to $300,000 a year, on the average, from DOL. In total our grants came to about $5 million. Mostly, the funding was for research and we were given a great degree of freedom in choosing our research targets. But we also did some training for DOL and ran some conferences. In addition, as far as government financing was concerned, we got some grants from Commerce and HEW and also some support from the New York City Planning Commission in the late 1960s.

From the outset, I have had good support from the foundations. In 1940, Joseph Willetts, vice president of the Rockefeller Foundation, offered Dean McCrea of Columbia's Business School research support for two faculty members, one senior and one junior. Dean McCrea picked James Bonbright and me to receive these funds. In later years, our research had varying support from most of the major foundations. Currently, with government cut-backs, we are almost solely dependent on foundation support.

When I first organized the Conservation of Human Resources group

in the late 1940s with the support of Eisenhower, he helped us raise
what were then relatively large sums from private corporations. Each of
ten corporations pledged $5,000 a year, for a minimum of five years.
The presidents were often Eisenhower's personal friends. We got
money from Cities Service, Coca-Cola, Standard Oil of New Jersey, General Electric, DuPont, and others. We felt quite rich in those years and
we were able to expand our staff.

Besides funding, I early recognized the importance of linkages, connections, networks both in government and outside. For example, in
1939, when I studied the unemployed in South Wales, my sponsor was
Thomas Jones, who had been secretary of the British Cabinet under
Baldwin and who later became head of the Pilgrim Trust. He set up
everything for me in the valleys without which help the research could
not have been carried through successfully. In Washington, I have had
good connections with many decision-makers. Over time my relationships and contacts expanded. I came to know well many of the top bureaucrats and senior congressional staff.

Another invaluable support for our research came about through the
establishment in 1951 by the Ford Foundation of the National Manpower Council at Columbia. The council had a most distinguished
group of members appointed by General Eisenhower. James D. Zellerbach of Crown Zellerbach was its first chairman, and when he was
appointed ambassador to Italy he was succeeded by Erwin Canham of
the *Christian Science Monitor*. This council over a ten-year period
brought major manpower issues to the attention of the American
public. There was interlocking staff between CHR and the council, and
our research was surely aided and abetted by the ability of the council
to help formulate public policy.

In such an extended research program as ours—forty-five years up to
the present—there have been a host of specific findings. It may be
worth singling out some of the *most general* findings. The most basic is
that ours is a human economy. Economists don't think properly about
human resources. Human resources are the basic factors in wealth creation. The fact that they call our system capitalism is a dead giveaway:
it's got the focus on the wrong element. We believe that it's not physical
and financial capital that are the most important inputs; but rather human resources.

Since the publication of Gary Becker's book on human capital in
1964, economists have been paying more attention to these matters.
Becker is in the main economics tradition and his framework has provided a basis for most of the current research on questions of human

capital. There has been a significant output from these efforts, but most of the work is too narrow from my point of view. In our research we pay close attention to the institutional setting within which human capital is created, developed, and utilized. That is not the case in conventional economics. We pay attention to the family, to education, to values, to work, to health, and to the broader social and institutional settings. This broader framework is more appropriate in our view than the more limited and abstract models of traditional economics.

Another basic finding from our research program is that there is a great waste of manpower and human resources in advanced industrial societies. I saw that first in our studies of the long-term unemployed and then again in the several volumes that we published on the experience of persons in the military in World War II. The waste stems from inadequate families, from inadequate schools, from poor performance of the economy in creating jobs. Another major source of waste is grounded in the pervasive discrimination against women and minorities.

Somewhere along the line I shifted my views as to the relative strengths of different intervening and corrective influences. I still believe that government at all levels is a potent instrument, but I can now see that it has severe limitations. If a person grows up in a dependent family and has poor schooling, it's hard for government to compensate for these basic deficits.

I might also say that some part of our general findings were unexpected. I started with a heavy psychological, individualistic emphasis. It became clear, for example, in the research that resulted in our three-volume work, *The Ineffective Soldier: Lessons for Management and the Nation,* that a person's ineffectiveness may not reflect his individual failings as much as system malperformance. In that study, we were able to pinpoint and prove system malperformance. A lot of the waste came about because of faulty military policies affecting recruitment and utilization of manpower. And in our book *The Negro Potential,* we pointed out that as late as 1955 there were no blacks employed in manufacturing in the Southeast except blast furnaces in the steel mills of Birmingham, Alabama, and in some lousy jobs in the southern saw mills. Such findings reflected on the system, not the individuals who were victimized. We also found great system malperformance and waste in the material presented in a book called *The American Worker in the Twentieth Century* (1963). It was a history through autobiographies of ordinary, run-of-the-mill workers. It illuminated the waste of human resources in the most vivid fashion imaginable.

In addition to these basic and general findings running through all our work, there were, of course, a lot of specific findings in each book and in our separate activities. For example, *The Unemployed* called attention to serious secondary effects of male unemployment on wife and children. It also highlighted the fact that most of the unemployed wanted to work, were not shirkers. As a result of three follow-up interviews, we discovered that most of the unemployed, except those who were severe alcoholics, made it back to work once the war boom got under way.

In our Welsh coal miners study, we showed the corrosive effects of mass unemployment not only on the lives of individuals but on communities and such institutions as the church. We also predicted, correctly as it has turned out, that once the miners did get work again, they would make collective bargaining in the United Kingdom a misery for management and the nation.

In my overseas travels on advisory missions, I always tried to help the countries I visited set up a manpower planning capability and establish more effective linkages between their educational systems and their emerging skill requirements. I also showed them how to strive after a better balance between their university output and their requirements for different kinds of professional personnel.

These are but a few examples of the specific findings and activities that made up the substance of our work. The basic findings I reported above are generalizations of these specific findings. Of course, once they appeared, they guided us to further specific findings and activities.

There were a number of ways, direct and indirect, in which our books had some influence on social policy. First of all, through our practice of writing and publishing books that reported our research and made recommendations for policy, we hoped to raise public consciousness about the waste of human resources. Reviews of our books in such widely circulated media as the *New York Times Book Review* were especially helpful in this regard. For example, the sociologist John Dollard wrote a first-page laudatory review of our three-volume work, *The Ineffective Soldier*. A review like that helped to communicate our general ideas widely. Since many of our books fell somewhere between popular writing and academic writing, they were not always reviewed in the popular, widely circulated journals. On the whole, we still felt justified in using books to disseminate our ideas to the public. I think our books didn't get much notice when they didn't fit the dominant ideology. For example, when my colleagues Hiestand and Rubens and I wrote a book called *The Pluralist Economy* (1964), which pointed out that more than one third of the American economy was in the public or nonprofit sector, a fact contrary to American ideology, the book was not widely noticed in the United States, even though it had a considerable success overseas, both in Europe and Asia.

Our research had a more direct effect on policy through federal legislation. Senator Joseph Clark of Pennsylvania, as chairman of a Senate subcommittee, held hearings in 1960 that explored national manpower and unemployment problems. The senator asked me to testify and later encouraged me to organize a group of senior academics to advise him. I did so and we met at the Harvard Club shortly after Kennedy took office. We suggested to Clark that new legislation require the President to submit an annual report on manpower and to fund an external research program in the Department of Labor. Both recommendations were accepted. I also played a role through congressional testimony when President Kennedy sent up his Civil Rights Act without an employment provision. Senator Clark encouraged several of us to testify on adding an unemployment section which was added in the final bill. Later on, as the chairman of the National Commission for Manpower Policy, I wrote reports on unemployment among youth and on a public sector employment program that President Carter in 1977 used as a basis of his new program.

Some of our influences on policy came about through the actions of special interest groups. For example, when I published *The Negro Potential,* the National Urban League asked me to do a series of speeches around the country on black unemployment. I think our research recommendations helped the league to push for policy reforms. When Patricia Harris was Secretary of HEW she told me that she had heard one of my Urban League speeches when she was a student and was instructed by it. I worked from time to time with other interest groups.

Of course, I worked closely with the existing government organizations, such as DOD, DOL, and HEW. But beyond these government agencies and the private interest organizations, some of our influence on manpower policy were realized in the private sector. For example, for over ten years I was active in a variety of ways at DuPont. Over a thousand of their bench scientists who were being converted into general managers were instructed by me in the problems of manpower, managing, and organization. I also interacted with many executives and with members of the executive committee. The DuPont relationship was the longest on-going relation I had with the private sector. But I had other opportunities for influence. I taught over many years at the Advanced Management Center of General Electric at Crotonville. And I always gave the major lecture on manpower at the advanced management program that our Business School ran at Arden House. Over a period of thirty years, with a hundred people coming each year from the major corporations, I had a good opportunity to communicate our findings and policy recommendations.

As I have indicated, we used several different modes to carry our research findings into the policy arena. Some of these that I haven't mentioned yet need to be spelled out. One mode of influence was to have our works purposefully distributed to the relevant groups of decision-makers. For example, when we were ready to publish *The Ineffective Soldier,* we arranged with the Pentagon to have a full day of meetings with all of the senior officials of the three major services to brief them on what we had found and its importance for their recruitment, training, and utilization policies. Even though the military finally didn't do much to change its policy, it paid attention to what we said and took some of what we said into account even if it didn't like our basic orientation.

Repeated testifying before congressional committees proved an important vehicle of influence. I estimate that over the last forty years I have probably testified before Congress not less than three times a year. We had a constant and continuing audience in Congress for our work.

I have already mentioned my briefing of Secretary of the Army Frank Pace. But I presented our research and policy recommendations to many other government officials as well, from presidents down to senior bureaucrats, the quasi-permanent civil servants who have a lot of influence on policy sooner or later. My speeches for the Urban League were a kind of briefing of the leaders and potential leaders of that organization. And in the private sector, I did a good deal of briefing of senior corporate executives.

Of course, we did a lot of communicating through the print media with the public and with special-interest groups. Over the last forty years, I would guess, I have had an average of about three telephone calls a week from the major newspapers and magazines, such as the *New York Times, Wall Street Journal, Business Week,* and *Fortune.* I am supportive of the press and glad to talk with them; on the whole, they handle what I tell them pretty well. However, I have little liking for, and have not done much with, television. Occasionally I do a short show, but I don't find television a satisfactory medium for explaining anything to anybody. Radio interviews are more successful and often provide more time to brief listeners.

We are often called upon to counsel organizations and people who

are writing on or having to act in the manpower arena. For a period
of ten years, for exampe, the State Department sent me all over the
world to counsel governments, universities, trade unions, and employer
groups. I've traveled to all the continents except Australia. One area
where my advice has been especially influential is Japan. In the late
1950s, Saburo Okita, a distinguished international economist who was at
that time chief economist in the prime minister's office and who later
became, for a brief time, foreign minister, came to my office at Columbia to explore with me what I was doing in research on human resources. He had heard about my book *Human Resources: The Wealth of
a Nation* (1958), which was based on lectures that I had given at the
University of California, Berkeley. He took my book back to Japan, translated it, and so, very early in the Japanese recovery, my policy orientation became available to the Japanese. Okita understood that a sustained
economic recovery in Japan would largely depend on what they did to
improve their human resources. I emphasized very strongly to him that
their educational system was inadequate for a long-term expansion. I
don't think our research and policy recommendations have ever had a
larger effect than they have had in Japan. Almost all of my books, including those on women, have been translated into Japanese. Despite
the common conception that the Japanese emphasize machines and
technology, they have pursued an aggressive human resources policy.
As it gets reported back to me, I have had a major influence on them.

Our group did a lot of advising overseas. I myself have never been
much interested in the big international organizations, such as OECD
and the European Economic Community, but more in individual countries with defined problems. I did do one major presentation for OECD
on employment (1973) but found the conference too slow-moving.
However, one of my senior colleagues in the Conservation of Human
Resources group, Dr. Beatrice Rubens, who has been a key member of
our staff for twenty years, is a respected American expert in the international community on human resources problems. The particular countries I myself have worked in have been the United Kingdom, Germany,
France, Italy, Israel, Iran before the revolution, India, and elsewhere in
the developing world—for example, Egypt, Ethiopia, and West African
countries, Afghanistan, and Indonesia.

Inevitably, we became an information center and intermediary for
many research and activist groups in the human resources arena. But
we never started a journal or engaged in formal graduate training. It
was all informal communication. We didn't even do that much publishing in the professional journals. We relied chiefly on publishing books.

One last mode of influence has been referred to earlier if only in passing. National committees and commissions can have a considerable effect on public policy. From 1962 to 1982, I was the chairman of the National Manpower Advisory Committee, the National Commission for Manpower Policy, and the National Commission for Employment Policy. The commissions were charged with preparing studies and policy recommendations for the President, Congress, and members of the cabinet. After each meeting, for example, I wrote a letter, which is now part of the public record, to all of the concerned parties about our discussions and recommendations. Unfortunately, most of the legislation under which we operated was focused on short-term palliatives rather than long-term rehabilitation of the unemployed and the poor. I like to think that many of our recommendations were helpful.

Like other long-term programs of research, we experienced a certain amount of indifference and resistance to our work. Some was intellectual, other resistance came on value conflicts, and some for still other reasons. *The Pluralistic Economy,* for example, ran against the grain of economists, who think of ours as primarily a private-sector economy. There was also major resistance from specialists to our book on occupational choice. It proved unsettling to many in vocational guidance and counseling. We showed that they were operating without any theoretical direction, on a hit-or-miss basis; they didn't really know what they were doing or where they were going. We started out reinforced by a review of the literature by Professor Donald Super, an expert in the field on the Teachers College faculty. But his old-time colleague at Teachers College, Kitson, was furious. Kitson wrote such an angry review of our book in the major journal that the editor was embarrassed and asked me to write a special article in reply. The people in educational psychology are still uneasy about me because I am criticizing them from outside their field. The younger generation is more relaxed and more accepting of our views. But still, they didn't like it when I wrote a book, at the request of the Rockefeller Brothers Fund, called *Career Guidance: Who Needs It? Who Wants It? Who Can Improve It?* (1971). Self-interest came into play. The guidance counselors at that point were looking to the federal government to provide large funds to expand their scope. But my *Career Guidance* was a severe indictment of the processes of career and school guidance and that didn't help them in Washington. I criticized the advice they were giving to black youngsters and to women. They were just steering these people into low-paying, segregated occupations.

I've also met resistance from many who rise to the top in large organizations, whether in the military or in the corporate world. These people believe themselves to be great experts in all matters of human resources. They feel that their achievement certifies that they know more about human resources than anyone else. They think that experience is a better guide than systematic knowledge. They can't accept the idea that systematic knowledge might be useful for strategic planning. We saw some of this resistance early when Eisenhower wrote to fifty captains of industry and other important people for support of our research work. He finally got the financing we needed, but mostly from personal acquaintances. Many of the leaders didn't answer, and some five or six chief executive officers were bold enough to write and say that the general's proposal didn't make any sense. Opposition to our work was stronger in the early days.

As I've said, so far as the top military leaders were concerned, I was in an ongoing fight with them over many years. I won an occasional skirmish, but I always lost the battle and surely the war. They remained masters in their own house. The last study I did for the military was for the Scientific Advisory Board of the Department of Defense. The DOD set up a blue-ribbon committee to look over all aspects of manpower policy in the armed services. We recommended (1971) that they make a great many changes in their policies. But the services buried our report, buried it so effectively that when Eliot Richardson became for a period secretary of defense, he couldn't get a copy from within the department. The military kept insisting, in contrast to our arguments, that they could use only what they called "quality" people. They said that higher standards of selection were all the more necessary because of the growing technological sophistication of their equipment. We felt each of the services was trying to outdo the other in attracting the "best" people. They had the simplistic notion that anybody who had not graduated from high school could not serve effectively in the military. I felt our position had been proved when President Johnson had earlier ordered Secretary McNamara to accept a couple of hundred thousand nongraduates. Analyses showed that these people performed satisfactorily. A high proportion, around 90 percent, made it in the military. But the top brass resisted, pointing to a few percentage points of higher early discharges among the nongraduates. We stressed that most nongraduates could make it even without special training. The difference between the best selectees and others was only a few percentage points. Accepting the latter would make for a more representative armed forces. Much of the resistance was directed to controlling the number of blacks. The military also resisted our recommendations for increased civilianization. They wanted most of their people to be in uniform.

Leaders in the private sector also often resisted our recommendations that they think more broadly about and make more use of the pool of available manpower. They felt that they should recruit only the best and that was the policy they were following. We told them that many good people didn't necessarily fit their prototype and that their selection procedures were pretty weak. Their job interviews were not much better than just taking anybody at random between the fifteenth percentile at the bottom and the tenth percentile at the top. We were convinced of this by our data on half a million cases of selection that we reported on in *The Ineffective Soldier.* We knew from these data about the softness of all selection criteria. And we also argued that performance was not just a matter of individual characteristics but of the organization of work. For example, we learned that what was important was to have sufficient work for everyone who is employed, and to avoid top-heavy staffs. Organizations should end each day with some work unfinished. That should usually be the least important work. When all work gets finished every day, there are probably too many people around. Again, I'm thinking in system terms about manpower and work.

The Human Economy (1976) is really the closest I have come to formulating a comprehensive approach to my more than four and a half decades of research. The book sets out the key aspects about how people develop their potential, the extent to which different societies further or hinder such developments, the importance of intermediary institutions such as the military, the influence of the labor market and economic development in creating job opportunities, the special steps that a society can take to broaden options for all people. In my prejudiced view, it represents a much broader approach than Becker's *Human Capital.* Admittedly, it does not lend itself so readily to quantitative exercises.

From my long experience in research and in social policy advising, I think I see a few general patterns with regard to the place of research in the policy process. The choices that Congress has at any particular time are narrowly defined by the existing political situation. Not everything is possible, no matter what the knowledge base. If the time is right "politically," then Congress can make use of whatever knowledge is available. It tends to do this primarily through its staffs, and the staffs do a pretty good job of eliciting what knowledge and research are available. The staffs are generally smart and energetic, but they are presented with different social science research findings and have the task of sorting out these differences. It's important for the social researcher to know how to present and interpret his particular findings. For example, I recently made a presentation at a two-day symposium on what to do about the Medicare Trust Fund. The meeting was organized by the Congressional Budget Office and the House Ways and Means Committee. Several different proposals were made at that meeting. Congress often finds a wide range of academic opinions on almost every issue: taxes, health, manpower, employment policy. Usually there is nothing definitive emerging from the research that would force Congress to move in a single direction. Congress can learn from different pieces of social science research, but finally it must rely on its own values and its assessment of the existing political situation. Social science research, thus, is only a part of the political process, one ingredient of the environment out of which the policy choices are made.

This is surely the case wherever large social and political values are at stake and also frequently when less weighty matters are being considered by particular organizations, like the military or a large corporation. Sometimes, in fact frequently, decision-makers don't want larger issues brought in. They are seeking narrow solutions. For example, the military usually sends social scientists narrow personal questions and expects them to come up with narrow answers. Large organizations don't want to be shaken up except when their top people themselves want to shake them up. Therefore, social scientists are usually kept on a tight rein. They can make suggestions about tactics, but not about strategy or overall reconfiguration of the organization. I should stress, however, that I don't want to exaggerate the power of even the top decision-makers to introduce changes. I've worked for nine presidents and I feel that they don't have as much power as is often attributed to them. It takes a very fluid situation in the country at large for the President to be able to exercise significant leadership. Everything is greatly constrained. There's a great deal of division of power in this country, all kinds of groups and subgroups, and the President usually doesn't have much leverage. On the whole, we get changes in the existing social structure only at times of crisis or after a big hold-up, as with civil rights in the 1960s. I've been impressed that power isn't what it seems to be. This is true also for private corporations. Just maintaining a complex organization is a difficult job. The golden age of the American corporation was from 1945 to 1950; chief executives could do a lot. But the conditions for the exercise of power, for establishing a basic new policy for an organization, are generally quite limited. There's a strong conservative force operating in all organizations.

All this indicates that I think social change is possible but not easy to come by. One of the most important generic influences for change are the factors that I've been concerned with throughout my research program—that is, broadening opportunity, increasing options for people, bringing new people into the system. A long spell of good employment opportunity is essential to bring this about. The job-creating capabilities of a society provide more of a return for change than anything else I know about. It's also essential, for expanding opportunity, to enlarge access to the educational system, all the way up. Educational access is important for employment opportunity. So we might say that new knowledge creates new machines and organizational proletariats and these expand economic development and employment opportunities. I think of society as a system of interacting factors in which all of these elements create the human economy which we must understand and which must be taken into account in all social policy.

For the future, I hope to be able to continue having the energy, talent, and luck I've had in the past in being able to spot new issues early in the human resources field. I like to think of myself as, one, the *ewige Student,* and, two, the exploratory surgeon who does the initial incision. I get excited by new problems, new data. And I hope to keep right on in this way.

Chapter Four

Morris Janowitz

Military Institutions, the Draft, and the Volunteer Army

Morris Janowitz, longtime and key member of the distinguished Department of Sociology at the University of Chicago, is the author of The Professional Soldier *and many other writings on the sociology of military institutions. This work not only founded and became the central theme of a new field of scholarly research but had a large influence on policy-making in the American military and on questions of the military draft and the volunteer army. For twenty-five years his work has been at the center of research and policy-making on the structure and processes of military institutions in the United States.*

Interview: Fall 1983

A lot of the influences on my professional formation and aspirations as a sociologist go back before I had any formal training in the field. In fact, I was a kind of working sociologist before I even began graduate work in sociology at the University of Chicago after the Second World War. The earliest influence came from my family, especially from my mother. My parents were émigrés, my father from Poland and my mother from Russia. My mother had left Russia in 1905 but kept up her interest and concern with what was going on there, as did many

of her fellow émigrés in Paterson, New Jersey, where we lived. My
mother's interest made me very much aware of the problems of political unrest and change in Europe. It also made me very wary of broad
social movements and efforts toward wholesale social change. This
wariness shows up in all my later work in macrosociology, in my work
on institution-building and social change.

When I went off to college, I didn't know what I wanted to do after-
ward. I majored in economics and was very much under the intellectual
and personal influence of the institutional economist Bruce Lannes
Smith. The philosopher Sidney Hook also had views that attracted me. I
didn't take any sociology courses when I was at the Washington Square
College of New York University. I began to think that if I majored in
economics I might get a job in some agency of the New Deal; that was
the time of the Depression, my college years. There was a very intense
intellectual and political discussion going on at NYU in those days, similar to that at the New School for Social Research and at City College,
but less vocal, and Smith got me a job at the New School collecting
tickets for a series of public lectures on the heated issues of the times. I
was especially impressed by the ideas of Harold Lasswell, the political
scientist from the University of Chicago. I was introduced to Lasswell by
Bruce Lannes Smith while still an undergraduate. Our first meeting, if I
remember correctly, was supper in a very elegant restaurant. Lasswell
saw himself as a talent scout for the social sciences and thrived on in-
troducing the talented graduate students to potential employers. I read
his work and became acquainted with him. He was to have a strong
influence on me. But I was not then very familiar with all the achievements of the Chicago School of Sociology. I was familiar only with the
W. I. Thomas massive study of Poles in Poland and Poles in the United
States.

I was graduated from NYU in 1941 and went to work as a research
assistant to Lasswell in his War Communications Project at the Library of
Congress in Washington. Some of it was dull work, going through files
of newspapers. But there were numerous social scientists working in
Washington at that time, both at the Library of Congress and elsewhere.
They were doing political, sociological, and psychological research on
the problems of the enemy and the war. I got into that culture. Some of
the people who were in Washington at that time and whom I knew or
knew about were Franz Neumann, the political scientist; Herbert Mar-
cuse; Otto Kirchheimer; a lot of them were German refugees who had
the advantage of knowledge of Germany. But there were also people
like Barrington Moore, who spent his after-war career at Harvard. Even-

tually, many of these people wound up doing current, contemporary social and political analyses for the Office of Strategic Services. I was especially interested in the more systematic analysis of propaganda that Lasswell was doing.

But mostly I was interested in getting closer to the war. In 1943 I entered the army as a private and did research on propaganda and morale, concentrating on the German army's problems. In 1944–45 I was in Europe and had the opportunity to do research on these matters at firsthand. I was really a participant observer. Later on, out of this experience came the article I did with Edward Shils, "Cohesion and Disintegration in the German Army in World War II" (1948), which I called my Wehrmacht study. This paper has been reprinted and cited a great deal. It was an early expression of my interest in the sociology of military institutions. Its emphasis on the importance of the effects of informal social relations among fighting men on their morale and fighting ability was one theme of my later work. Men fought for their buddies more than for ideology. I came out of the army a second lieutenant with a Bronze Star and a Purple Heart. The war had put its mark on me.

After the end of the war, I stayed in the army for a while, but I wanted to go to graduate school in sociology. Various people in Washington were urging me to do so. Some of these people were from Harvard and suggested I go there. I went up to see Talcott Parsons, and I found that interesting, but I wasn't moved by that place and its imagery. I decided to go to Chicago for a number of reasons. I knew Lasswell, of course, and expected to find his imprint there in the political science department. I didn't, as it turned out. Also, I had come to know Edward Shils; he wanted me to come, and when I went I did some work with him. There was an exceptionally able group of fellow graduate students at Chicago after the war: Albert Reiss, Eleanor Sheldon, Ralph Turner, Natalie Rogoff (Ramsoy), and Dudley Duncan. I worked mostly with the German refugee Bruno Bettelheim, who had become head of the Orthogenic School at Chicago. He invited me to join him in his study of the social origins of race and ethnic prejudice. Out of that work we published my first book, *The Dynamics of Prejudice*. Bettelheim and I became good friends but after that I worked on the research that became my first independent book, *The Community Press in an Urban Setting* (1952). I had a powerful interest in continuing my work on military organizations, and I pursued my interests privately. In sociology the study of the military was, at that time, viewed with suspicion and reservation. While I was at the University of Chicago in the years immediately after the war, I kept my interest in the field of military organizations rather quiet. I was appointed an assistant professor in the College at Chicago in 1948, but I thought I had little chance to stay there in the long run. So when I was offered a position at the University of Michigan in 1951, I went there.

That was where I published *The Professional Soldier*. I didn't have any special theoretical or methodological purpose in writing this book. I just felt I had a job to do, to understand the military, why men fight. It was an enlargement of the problem I had dealt with in the Wehrmacht study. I felt I was dealing with a very practical problem and I wanted to do a readable book but not a popular one. The central problem I dealt with required some sophistication, some concern with sociological theory, but not much. In our German study, we had emphasized the use of intensive interviews to get at the German soldiers' morale and reasons for fighting. In this book I used whatever theory and whatever data and methods I could find to help me do the job. I used historical materials, interviews, survey data, everything. In this study, I had to dig in deeper, use a combination of methods. I don't believe there should be a sharp differentiation of the organization of research between applied and basic. I believe the more you have this differentiation, the less effective your work is in making policy.

Of course, my values were deeply involved in this work. As long ago as when I was in high school I had come to feel that we were going to have to fight the Germans. It was for that reason that I studied German in high school. My leftist acquaintances used to call me a premature anti-Fascist. My long-term objective was a peaceful world order. I knew we couldn't have a peaceful world by coercion alone. But I also knew that some coercion or force was necessary. I wanted to understand the nature of legitimate force such as was embodied in the military, how it might contribute to a peaceful world. I felt one could not contribute to conflict among nations unless one understood the military. I had learned that the British and French have an intuitive knowledge of the nature and uses of the military as a result of their long experience with wars and armies. In the United States, in contrast, we were much less understanding, more inconsistent about dealing with armed forces. We built them up for wars, then destroyed them when the wars were over, then built them up again for new wars. It was all so wasteful and pointless.

My specific policy goals were to increase public knowledge of the military but also to increase the military's knowledge of itself. I have always believed that social science research served as a teaching device, a way of helping people to be more reflective. I think my main book on the professional soldier has been successful in achieving such goals. And all my later work on the military has really just been a continuation of my original purpose: to help in dealing with what is a very practical problem for our country and for the world as a whole.

My book was written with very small funding resources. The foundations were very important for this work. When Bernard Berelson was director of the Behavioral Sciences Division at the Ford Foundation, he had the funds to give a certain number of people grants of $5,000. I was awarded one of these grants and that let me do what I wanted to, which was my book on the military. I also got support from the Russell Sage Foundation. Donald Young was then the president and Leonard Cottrell was his chief colleague there. I worked especially with Cottrell. But Young had had the idea of having Russell Sage bring social science to the working professions. Young and Cottrell were commissioning small studies, published as pamphlets, of sociology and these different professions: medicine, law, social work, etc. I did a pamphlet on the sociology of the military establishment. That was part of my work for *The Professional Soldier*. My work was done on a shoestring. I have never sought any federal money for my work on the military. I did, of course, get small sums sometimes for giving a lecture or doing one or two days of consulting, but I never took any research funds from the Department of Defense. Partly it was because too much red tape and paperwork was involved, but even more it was because of the objections of my university students and colleagues to connections with DOD. *The Professional Soldier* was a one-man effort. I did not have a staff of graduate students, let alone research assistants. I employed for a couple of months a graduate student who was interested in a cohort of military officers in the armed forces. The goals of this particular effort were to probe the actual profession and to dig deeper into the differences between different levels of the officer corps. I did not even have the assistance and support of my colleagues in the social sciences, and especially in sociology. I had strong assistance from my sociological colleagues at the University of Michigan in other topics where our work overlapped. But they were not interested in research and writing on the military, and had little substantive knowledge upon which I could draw. I received help from some military historians who were intrigued by my efforts. There were a few political scientists who were interested, but only a few. It was clear to me that the tasks of developing a "behavioral" approach could not be limited to one or two universities. But it was also clear to me that interest in the topic would grow rapidly. Instead of a few universities developing core efforts, the most likely development would be a national network, scattered throughout universities and in institutions devoted to research. My first effort in this regard was to hold a meeting in the mid 1950s in Michigan to which about ten interested social scientists from different universities came; the number grew rapidly, so that by the early 1980s I had identified nine hundred persons who had developed a stake in the study of armed forces and society, in the United States and on a comparative basis as well.

After my book was published and was very successful, I got some continuing support for work in this field from both the Ford and Russell Sage Foundations. Most of this money, especially the sums from the Ford Foundation, approximately $40,000 a year, was not directly for me but for the study group which I started in this field, the Inter-University Seminar on Armed Forces and Society, of which I was the chairman from 1961 to 1980. Compared to the grants in mainstream sociology, the sums were indeed small. The money wasn't for research but to hold meetings, discuss and criticize one another's work, and to run a journal. Once in a while I'd get a very small amount of money from some interested businessman, nothing much. There were no professional associations to fund my work.

The body of propositions explored in *The Professional Soldier* can be summarized in terms of the following five hypotheses. For each of the five propositions there is a body of supporting data—biographical, literary, survey, historical, comparative. We are dealing with the case of the United States during the period around 1950. Here are the five propositions, which later became the central hypotheses or themes for our new subdiscipline: (1) There has been a change in the basis of authority, a shift from authoritarian domination to greater reliance on manipulation, persuasion, and group consensus. (2) There is a narrowing skill differential between military and civilian elites. The new tasks of the military require that the professional soldier develop more and more of the skills and orientations common to civilian administrators and civilian leaders. (3) There has been a shift in officer recruitment. The military elite has been undergoing a basic social transformation since the turn of the century. These elites have been shifting their recruitment from a relatively narrow high social status to a broader and broader base more representative of the population at large. (4) Patterns of career development in the military change. Both specialized training and general education increase in importance and in the length of time given to them for satisfactory professional development. Innovative behavior is more necessary and more valued. Officers who display such behavior, the so-called adaptive leaders, are more likely than traditional type officers to reach the highest rungs of the professional hierarchy. And, finally, (5) the older doctrine of absolutism is replaced by a more democratic, pluralistic, pragmatic ideology for both the career and the missions of the military. This proposition was the opposite of C. W. Mills' notion, developed in *The Power Elite,* that the military is a powerful and anti-democratic institution. It was also in opposition to Samuel Huntington's view, proposed in his *The Soldier and the State,* that the military can be successful only if it is in clear-cut distinction from the civilian world. My proposition is that pluralistic doctrine leads to more harmonious civil-military relations. Of course, not all elements of the older traditionalism disappear from the military; some remain functional even in the modern world. But the trend to the new type of military is strong and prevailing if not total and wholly inevitable.

There were a number of integrated findings in my book. First, there was the historical account of the transformation of the military from its earlier character as a closed, isolated group with "heroic," feudal traditions into a group of modern professionals who were heterogeneous in their social origins and more open to the society around them. I found that a broad base of recruitment from the larger society was necessary to avoid having the military turn inward on itself, on its own loyalties, become isolated from the rest of the society, and come to feel itself in opposition to other groups and interests. I found that it would be desirable to partly "civilianize" the military, that is, to enlarge its civilian duties and overcome its "heroic" imagery. I coined the term "constabulary role" to describe the new image and functions that I thought would be central for the modern American military. A "constabulary force" is a military organization that is prepared to act at any time, that is committed to a minimum use of force to achieve its ends, and that seeks viable, steady-state international relationships rather than a "final" victory. It assumes a protective rather than an aggressive military posture. The major dilemma of such a force is that its success lies in its ability to prevent war while being always ready to fight.

But I didn't feel that the military, any more than any other profession, should be dominated by outsiders. I felt they should have their own leadership and intellectual leaders, to understand and develop their new function and role. Such a leadership would see the necessity for limited rather than "heroic" and unlimited warfare.

The main thing that surprised me in our findings and analysis was the degree of civilianization of the military that seemed necessary for it to be effectively integrated into modern society. I had thought I would find the military more differentiated from the rest of society. The extent to which it had to adapt to modern society was unexpected. I was not only surprised but pleased by the finding. I favor the greater integration of the military into the whole society.

My book immediately aroused a lot of discussion both in the military itself and in the attentive publics in Congress and elsewhere. A little before my book appeared, Samuel Huntington published another book on the military; it's a pretty conservative book; mine is more pragmatic. The two books started a dialogue which has continued up to the present, not only between Huntington and me but among other people. The military was especially interested in the findings and argument of my book. It became and has remained standard and required reading at various military training establishments: for example, West Point, the Naval Academy, the Air Force Academy, the War College. We have sold more than fifty thousand copies of that book. It has some influence on the conception that the American military has of itself and of its place in our society. It has also influenced personnel policies. It has taken a long time, but now the military is moving away from its policy of assignment of lone individuals to a policy of allocation and assignment of integrated groups. This is the practice of the French and British and it makes their armies more effective. Group assignment, and not assignment of individuals to particular tasks, is now a basic principle of military manpower management. The military also follows the recommendations that their leadership should have a broad set of learning experiences and a broad range of actual professional experiences. They are moving from "heroic," charismatic leadership to a more rational leadership principle. They have taken seriously the idea of the citizen-soldier. In addition, our social research played a part in the discussion over the legislation that ended the draft and set up a voluntary army. I was opposed to the voluntary army, but our work made it easier to make that policy work, to make it part of the American scene. On behalf of my views, I have testified several times before the Senate Armed Services Committee and also to the National Advisory Commission on Selective Service.

My work fed pretty directly into the concerns and views of a lot of existing interest groups which are concerned with civil-military relations, quasi-military service groups like the Air Force Association. These groups produce a lot of publications, do public relations, testify before the Congress, and the like. They're always quoting *The Professional Soldier* or other works by me and my associates. My work has become an essential part of the debate on the military's manpower policies. It has helped people to think in other than clichés, in more systemic, and more socioeconomic ways about policies. Even when people didn't come out with my answers, they certainly had to address the questions that my book and later work raised. They had to cope with the basic notions of civilianization, citizen-soldier, constabulary functions. We constructed new ways of stating the problem. Our influence has been pervasive and extensive.

A lot of the influence of my book has been indirect, so to speak, in the educational setting, not in the immediate and specific policy situation.

Personnel at the military education institutions were required to read the book, discuss it, learn its general findings and analysis. It gave them some general understanding of their identity and problems. The book also was relevant later, when military officers found themselves in specific policy situations. Civilians had more specific influence by testifying before congressional committees, especially the Armed Forces Committee when it was considering personnel problems. Our work had a large role in the discussion of the draft and the volunteer army. People like Sol Tax and Milton Friedman were on the other side and of course they prevailed, but my views played their part. In addition, whenever I lectured to the military, and I did a lot of that, I was not only presenting findings and analysis but putting out policy recommendations. As for the mass media, I was frequently being interviewed and quoted on military manpower problems. The media reflected a lot of public interest in these problems. I've even done a little bit of quasi-journalism myself, "editorial" and Op-Ed kinds of pieces setting forth my views.

Like other academics, I have done a lot of advising of other academics and of military professionals who were researching or writing in this field. I had office hours on the telephone; after eight o'clock people called me to talk about their work and ideas and activities. More formally, I trained a number of students, people who have made their career in the field and who in turn have trained students. At first I tended to discourage civilian students who wanted to specialize in this field because I thought there wasn't much academic or other career demand for it, but lately there have been more opportunities for people with such specialization. Not just graduate students but even some post-doctoral people who have become interested in the field have come to me for instruction and help.

The influence of my book and my work has spread through the formation of the Inter-University Seminar on Armed Forces and Society, which I have already mentioned. I founded it in the mid-fifties at Michigan as an informal working group, with members from Chicago and various other universities. That informal group was called the Inter-University Seminar on Military Organization; we renamed it later when we saw it had a broader scope than just military organization. When I moved to Chicago in 1960, that became its headquarters. We wanted it to be a professional association entirely independent of both the military and the government. We wanted it to be a collegial meeting place for scholars from everywhere; we financed it with funds from the Russell Sage and Ford Foundations, small funds. At the present, we have about a thousand members, including academics from various disciplines, civilian experts, and those military professionals who want to study themselves in a scholarly way. Its interdisciplinary character is very important to us. We have established our own journal, *Armed Forces and Society,* of which I have been the editor for about twenty years. We also have a newsletter, biennial conferences of the whole association, and even various regional suborganizations with their own meetings. It has become the most important focus of the networks of those who specialize in the social science of military affairs.

One of the tasks that the Inter-University Seminar has had to work out over the years has been the main themes of the work in our field. On the whole, it has been my book and Samuel Huntington's *The Soldier and the State* which have been at the center of this thematic task. We have finally set out three major areas of research: civil-military relationships; the institutional, that is, the organizational and professional aspects, of military establishments; and the nature of armed conflicts. We have not been much interested in strategy, military history, or international relations; those are cultivated by other specialists.

The seminar has also had the job of deciding what the main issues and conceptual tools of our specialty were. We wanted to be a thoroughly scientific specialty, using the best scientific methodology, and claiming legitimacy on scientific grounds. Of course, the seminar also had to do what other professional associations do, namely, make the new specialty visible in the academic world, get it legitimated as a reputable discipline in the "academic market," so that funds and jobs would be available. We promoted ourselves not only through our own meetings but also through arranging sessions on our work at the various national and international social science associations. Out of our work came a great many articles and about twenty-five books that were published in *The Series on Armed Forces and Society.* We also publish an annual, *The Series on War, Revolution, and Peacekeeping.* Our journal is now a quarterly. Some people have compared it, for its importance to our field, to the *Archiv für Sozialwissenschaft* for Max Weber's work and to the *Année Sociologique* for Durkheim's work. Journals of this kind are very important for getting a new field started, for spreading its theories and research, and for serving as a focus for the new institution that builds up around a new field. Our journal was the first one devoted entirely to the social science analysis of the military and it has remained the pre-eminent one. It has distinguished editorial and advisory boards to guide it. The articles tend to have theoretical point and are always based on research. That research employs all the methodologies now available to social science. Comparative materials are very frequently present.

When *The Professional Soldier* was published in 1960, it was a considerable surprise to many of my academic colleagues. There was hardly any sociology of military institutions at that time. Most social scientists are liberals, and they felt something was morally wrong not only with the military but with studying it and with saying it had an important place in society. Later on in the sixties, at the time of student rebellions, my work on the military was criticized by sociology graduate students as being in favor of militarism and even imperialism. The question of the nature and uses of the military arouses strong values in many people; they want peace and they object to anything connected with coercion and violence. There were various kinds of resistance to my book and subsequent work on the military. Although my writings, on the whole, were viewed favorably by the military, there were, however, some military people, anti-intellectual types, who felt that their experience and intuition were better than what they defined as my mere speculation. They were the people who felt that only those inside the military could really understand it. And, finally, there were other scholars, notably Samuel Huntington, who had objections that were a mixture of intellectual and value factors. Huntington disagreed with my concept of the "citizen-soldier" and my argument for the importance of this type in a democratic society. He felt that the military should continue its old traditions and remain a conservative element in society. But the dialogue between his position and mine have provided a useful focus for a lot of the subsequent work in the field. Recently he has changed his position somewhat. Our relations have always been friendly despite our value-intellectual difference.

As a citizen-sociologist, if I may coin another term, I've learned many lessons from my research and writing and policy involvement about the military. Speaking in military terms, I have learned that sociology has to be a staff, and not a line, profession. We are, essentially, researchers and teachers, not decision-makers. There is a role for our work in society, and there is another role for the administrator or decision-maker who has been educated into some sort of social science understanding of the system or organization he is dealing with. Sociology should be instructive both for the decision-makers and for the alert public who participate indirectly in decision-making. Sociology has a lot to do in clarifying what the questions are people have to answer and decide, not with answering specific questions. I opt for what I call the "enlightenment model" for social science. I like to emphasize the voluntarism of social action and decision-making. I don't like the rigid determinism of some econometric and sociological models.

My work on the military has also convinced me of the existence, in modern industrialized societies like the United States, of considerably dispersed social and political power. I don't agree at all with Mills' ideas about the existence of a concentrated power elite running society. In fact, instead of having a tiny, manipulative elite running society, the power problem really is that there's so much pluralism and dispersion that it's hard to organize and integrate power for effective societal decision-making. Even in the military, where there is less dispersion, there is still a difficulty in getting power organized. A pluralistic democracy requires more effective and integrated power than is now often the case. I have tried to make this point in one of my recent books, *The Last Half Century*.

Finally, my work on the military and its personnel policies has taught me that it's not easy to get effective social change. Changing and building institutions is slow; you cannot create them *de novo;* you have to do a lot of muddling through to get any kind of change. Sociology and its research can help to enlighten the trial-and-error process of institution-building. While citizen participation, local involvement, and trial-and-error institution-building are all part of the process of democratic social change, still, the federal government must be the main source of change in American society. It's the only place where the necessary integration of dispersed interests and power can come from. In such a complex society as we have, the federal government must take the initiative in institution-building on many fronts, not try some sudden and sweeping change. And in all this, if it is to be successful and use the research findings and analysis of social science, it will have to have the cooperation of its citizens in the schools, the local communities and the work place, and the military.

Comprehensive Income Taxation

Joseph A. Pechman, until his recent retirement from that position, was a longtime director of economic studies at the Brookings Institution. In and out of government, he has spent most of his professional career in Washington, close to those who make economic policy for the federal government. As a specialist in the economics of taxation and government finance, a very large part of his work has been devoted to research and policy on comprehensive income taxation. He is also the co-originator of the Heller-Pechman revenue sharing plan. When taxation is the issue, Pechman is one of the few experts most likely to be called on to advise.

Interview: January 1983

I was an undergraduate in City College, New York, in the 1930s; I came from a poor family and was very much a child of the Depression. At City College I was a member of the group of students who were interested in social problems and argued about democracy, socialism, and communism. Many of those people later became academics and intellectuals; some of them, but not I, have become neoconservatives. At City College I was trained in mathematics and statistics. I worked for the WPA as a statistician and was attracted to the study of economics partly because of my interest in mathematics and statistics and partly because of my interest in social problems. There were many other people like me, people who went into economics out of mathematics and statistics. Economics was just becoming a lot more mathematical.

I went to the University of Wisconsin for my graduate work because it was known as a very good school and because they gave me a fellowship. Wisconsin was known then chiefly for its emphasis on institutional economics, but I wasn't especially interested in that. Wisconsin was a very congenial place. There were a great many progressive people on the faculty and among my fellow students. I realized early on that I was in economics because I was interested in social policy and in improving the welfare of people. Wisconsin was a good place for that kind of person. It was the home of the LaFollettes and their Progressive Party.

My training in public finance was taken under Professor Harold Groves, who was an eminent tax practitioner and theoretician in the twenties and thirties at the University of Wisconsin. At one time he had also been tax commissioner for the State of Wisconsin. Harold had a group of able young graduate students when I was there from 1937 to 1941, people like Walter Heller, Jess Berkhead, Richard Good, and Herbert Klarman. We learned from one another. It was during that period that my basic views on taxation were developed. I wrote a paper on the future of the Wisconsin income tax in which I estimated what Wisconsin could get from an effective income tax after the Depression was over. I remember that Groves and other people were shocked when I estimated what were then, apparently, huge yields from the income tax because of its high elasticity.

I was absent from economics entirely for about four and a half years during World War II. But right after the war, at the suggestion of Walter Heller, I joined what is now the Office of Tax Analysis in the Treasury Department. I became the assistant director, in charge of research on the individual income tax. Thus, for a number of years I was the inside expert on the individual income tax and further developed my ideas. When I left the Treasury to go into academic life and later to the staff of Brookings, my interest in income taxation continued and I developed a great many ideas on the basis of my Treasury experience.

In Groves I had a model of someone who was interested in both the theory and practice of public finance and income taxation. Although I was one of the more technical people at Wisconsin because I knew mathematics and could handle economic theory, still I was very much interested in applied research. Wisconsin was better for that than for theory. I was interested mainly in practical economics from the very beginning. I guess what I got from Groves was a keen interest in using the tax system to promote social objectives. That's why I was interested in taxation.

My interest in the theory of national income measurement and income taxation derived from a set of mixed factors—theoretical, practical, and methodological. I might give a little historical background here. For over a century, economists, starting with the classical English economists, knew what national product was and wrote about it. But it was not until the twentieth century that any measurement of national income was even tried. These attempts at measurement started as early as the 1920s at the National Bureau of Economic Research, which was then a new organization for the empirical and quantitative collection and study of economic data. The work on the measurement of national income was the result of the efforts of people like Wesley C. Mitchell and Simon Kuznets. For his work on national income measurement, Kuznets was eventually given the Nobel Prize. In the 1930s, probably as a result of the Depression, there was great interest in developing a systematic series of accounts that would yield estimates of the national income and its distribution. This work was later carried on at the Department of Commerce by George Jaszi, Ed Dennison, Milton Gilbert, and Charles Schwartz.

Against this background, I was interested as a graduate student in both national income accounting and public finance. At the end of my first year of graduate study, I did an M.A. thesis on national income produced in the manufacturing industries in Wisconsin. So my interest in national income started very early. The basic thrust of my work ever since has been to apply measurements to what is known in the economic literature as the Haig-Simons definition of income. When I was a graduate student, we all learned as a matter of course what the definition of income for tax purposes should be. But, rather interestingly, until I did it in the 1950s, nobody had actually used the available data to make even a ballpark estimate of what the Haig-Simons definition of income would actually yield.

I did not arrive at my ideas or theories about comprehensive income taxation right away. It was a derivative of my concern for making real measurements of the definition of income following the theoretical definition. I was absolutely amazed at the results. When I was able to compare the amounts you get from the theoretical definition of income and the amounts that are reported on tax returns, I found very, very large differences. That was what got me going on the need for tax reform and a new tax policy.

It wasn't any special new methodology that permitted me to make

these measurements. Whatever there was of new methodology had
been developed earlier in the work on the national income accounts. I
just happened to know of these new data and how to apply them to an
interesting applied problem. Marrying the two interests was not difficult.
The statistical techniques in what I've done are simple. Even in later
years, when I've used computers, the computers were used largely to
do arithmetic rather than to perform fancy new calculations. I was just
putting together theory and measurement.

As I've already indicated, mixed up with theoretical and methodological concerns of mine were certain value judgments. I was never a
Marxist, even though many of my early contemporaries were. But one
of my major goals always was to improve the welfare of people as a
whole, particularly people who are disadvantaged and poor. I came
from a household which in the 1930s was very, very poor. And I guess
that conditioned my outlook for the rest of my life. Equity and equal
opportunity have always been important norms for me. Of course, as
an economist I also value the norm of efficiency. But many of my colleagues in economics neglect equity entirely.

My views about equity and efficiency are summed up extremely well
in Arthur Okun's book of that title. He pointed out that the government
ought to modify the results of a free enterprise system in the interest of
making sure that the disadvantaged are not oppressed and do much
better than they might otherwise do. There is a trade-off between equity
and efficiency. At what level you modify efficiency is a value judgment.

But I'm not a radical economist in the sense that I would overturn
the private enterprise system. For example, I tend to agree with those
who would deregulate the system much more than we have up to now.
What is different about my views, I find, is that most economists wish
taxation would go away because it interferes with efficiency. As a result
they pay little attention to the equity effects of taxation, only to its economic or efficiency effect. They set taxation aside because it drives a
wedge between the results of the market system and what the individual or firm gets out of it. In the extreme, if you're a Hayekian for example, you would argue that the results of the free enterprise system—
unchanged by government and government tax policies—are morally
the correct results.

One of the reasons I was attracted to working at Brookings and why
Brookings, I suppose, was attracted to me is that we have mutual interests in promoting improvements in public policy. Brookings prides itself on being a policy-oriented organization. I think it's to Brookings'

credit that it has supported my work on tax policy for so long. Many other institutions might not have done that. Before I came to Brookings of course, my research was supported for some six and a half years by the government, while I was working in the Treasury Department just after World War II. Although I can now see that I was laying the background for being an expert in individual income taxation, that was very practical work and I did not publish widely. In fact, I didn't publish anything on this subject while I was an employee of the Treasury. The early part of my research, the articles I published in the 1950s, I did on my own. When I spent an academic year at MIT in 1953–54, I had the usual university support. Later, my work was supported by the Committee for Economic Development, which had an interest in tax reform. But both the MIT and the CED support were minor—relatively small amounts of money and other resources were involved.

The big change in resources for my work occurred when I came to Brookings and organized what is now known as Studies in Government Finance. It was then that outside funds became important. Initially, the Studies in Government Finance was supported by a grant of two million dollars from the Ford Foundation to Brookings. Of course, only a small part of that sum went for my personal research. It was used for all kinds of research and policy work. That program, in the long run, produced something like fifty books, hundreds of articles, and dozens of graduate students. These resources had a very large effect on the whole profession.

When I started to use the computer in my work, I had assistance from the Ford money. Later, I received support again from the government, this time from the National Science Foundation. Throughout this whole period, in addition to the outside funds, the Brookings Institution was supporting me from its general funds. Some of those general funds came from the endowment, some from the Ford Foundation, and some from other foundations. Both of the presidents of the Ford Foundation in my time, Henry Heald and McGeorge Bundy, approved the orientation of Brookings, to improve social policy in general and finance and tax policy in particular. The program officer at the Ford Foundation most interested in this work was Marshall Robinson, who was himself an economist.

I've never received any financial support from groups other than the foundations. There are many nonprofit organizations in the field of taxation; they come and go. Most of them do not seem to be financially viable. Many of them exist because one or two or a few people get religious about taxation. They come to me for intellectual support and for data. But I've never been financed by any of those organizations, even though I regard myself as a friendly supporter of their policy objectives.

I am constantly invited by business organizations and trade associations to talk to them, even though most of them disagree with my views. In some cases I get a fee for the talks, sometimes not. These groups want to hear what I think; they follow my work carefully even though they may not be sympathetic to my policy views. They want to know what the enemy is thinking and doing in the tax policy field.

I've already anticipated what some of the chief policy-relevant findings of my research are; let me make them explicit. The first major finding is that the income tax laws, as they have developed in the United States, have never taxed or even approached taxing all income. From the very beginning, there have been major departures from the definition of income that I consider appropriate for income taxation. And let me emphasize what I have made clear in all my writings and that a lot of people simply disregard. I feel strongly that there was no malice aforethought in all this, no conspiracy on the part of capitalists to gut the income tax, not to pay any income tax. The departures from the theoretical definition of income benefit people in all classes.

The second major finding is that, as a result of all those departures from the theoretical definition, it is clear that if we taxed all income and allowed a few necessary deductions, the present income rates would generate much more revenue for the federal government.

The third finding is, therefore, that we could use the additional revenue to reduce the tax rates across the board. My original estimate in the first article that I wrote on this subject, published in the *National Tax Journal* in 1955, was that we could reduce the rates, which then went up to 90 percent, by a third. In the late 1950s I increased my estimate of the possible rate reduction to 40 percent and that 40 percent estimate has held since that time. It held even after we began using computers to make the calculations; we get the same result that I got when I literally did the calculations on the back of an envelope.

As a result of these findings, my major policy effort has been to try to educate people to know that, because of all the departures from the theoretical definition of income, the income taxes are not nearly as punitive as they seem when you simply look at the marginal tax rates. We could improve the income tax situation simply by taxing income and reducing the tax rates. I have never used this line of argument to say that we should increase the progressivity of taxes, or decrease it. My purpose has always been neutral, to point out that whatever degree of progressivity the government wants, my method can get it better than the present one. I call this the comprehensive income tax approach.

The so-called flat income tax, about which there has been a lot of discussion lately, is just one of the alternative possibilities under the general approach of comprehensive income taxation. Many of the people who are behind the flat income tax understand that. They understand that the basic structure they are supporting is comprehensive income taxation, and therefore they view me as an ally. But as long ago as 1972, in an article written with Ben Oakder, we explicitly found that the flat income tax at the federal level would redistribute the tax burden from high to low and middle income recipients. The difference between the people who want the flat income tax and me is that I want a modest degree of rate graduation and they don't. The flat tax would greatly reduce the tax burden on the people with very high incomes in this country. I don't think there's any doubt of that.

There wasn't too much that was surprising to me in these findings. The most unusual finding was that the departures from a standard definition of economic income that were incorporated into the original 1913 tax, let alone all those that have been added since, were very big and benefited people at all income levels. I was not prepared for that result. I thought at that time that most of those "loopholes," as they are called in everyday language, would be loopholes only for the rich. If I had thought more deeply about it, I might have understood that right off, before the research. But it's the figures that hit you, and the specific departures. When I started my research we didn't tax unemployment compensation at all; we still don't tax social security benefits, except for those with very high income, though that may change; we have huge tax breaks for homeowners; and there are other examples. The existence of departures at all levels was more unexpected by me than the lack of comprehensiveness.

My research has exerted its effects on policy-making in a number of different ways. Probably the major vehicle was the articles and testimony that I have submitted to Congress, at the request of the several committees that have to do with tax policy. Over the years I have been invited by such influential committees as the Joint Economic Committee, the House Ways and Means Committee, the Senate Finance Committee, and the two Budget committees. All those committees have been interested in my research. I have also had influence through my more widely read published books and articles. The attention these have received has probably been increased by my connection with Brookings. The books and articles it publishes itself or that it sponsors have consid-

erable prestige because of their source. People come to talk to me all
the time, of course.

As for the general public—that is, those who read newspapers and
certain magazines—I am periodically visited by newspaper men and
women. Frequently young reporters, who have heard one of my statements on tax policy or who have heard about tax loopholes in other
places, come to me for an explanation. They have written a great many
articles about my positions on income tax policy. In the 1960s, I persuaded *Fortune* magazine to support comprehensive income taxation;
they wrote a long article describing and recommending it. That all happened because a writer from *Fortune* magazine had come down to get
my views on tax policy. He was persuaded enough to get his editor to
support my views. As for a super-mass audience, I once almost got an
article expounding my views in the *Reader's Digest*. But I didn't, and
that's a story I'll have to tell more about later when I describe the various kinds of resistance there have been to my particular views.

The press and the magazines pick up ideas on taxation very readily.
They know that almost everyone is interested in taxation because it af-
fects them so much and so directly. This interest increases greatly, it
erupts, when people get mad at the tax system. Taxation and tax policy
are interesting parts of economics because they are always current.
Even when it's not especially relevant, the public is likely to think that
taxes are the culprit for our ills. Of course, that's not true, but it's the
way people feel and think. So quite often there is a renewed interest in
tax reform. That's the time that I get called upon to testify before Congress and when my views are solicited.

Some of the changes in income taxation in recent years have been
foreshadowed in my research and recommendations. For example, we
have made some progress in expanding the tax base by removing certain deductions. All excise taxes—on alcohol, tobacco, automobiles, and
other commodities—were at one time deductible. Those were eliminated some time ago. More recently, we eliminated the deductions for
the gasoline tax, which I had said was unnecessary, although that happened primarily because of the oil crisis. Capital gains have received
favorable treatment in income tax policy at some times, less preferential
treatment at other times. This tax is, of course, a major economic and
political issue. So far the Congress hasn't gone as far as I would like
them to go, which is to tax capital gains as ordinary income and reduce
tax rates overall.

I even have recommended taxation of unemployment compensation.
This appalls my friends in the labor movement; they think I'm a terrible

reactionary in supporting this kind of income taxation. Yet they have no answer to my question: "Do you think it's fair for a person with $15,000 in wages to pay a higher tax than another person with $10,000 in wages and $5,000 in unemployment compensation?" That's exactly what happens; this differential tax exists. Of two people with the same income, the one with the unemployment compensation pays less tax. Although we still don't tax unemployment taxation in full, recently we have come to tax it if people have other income above a certain minimum: $12,000 for single people and $18,000 for married people.

The same principle is now being applied to social security benefits. Beginning in 1984, half of the benefits are taxed if the recipient has another income of $25,000 for single persons and $32,000 for married couples. Ultimately, these thresholds for unemployment compensation and social security benefits will be removed, I hope.

My research and ideas have had an indirect effect, or rather an interactive effect, with other reasons for reducing unnecessary tax deductions. When the congressional committees or the Treasury Department start thinking about taxation, perhaps to cut the deficit, they automatically turn to the kinds of lists that I used to draw up of the eroding features of the income tax laws. These lists, now called "Tax Expenditures," are a direct descendant of my original calculations. The Tax Equity and Fiscal Responsibility Act of 1982 had a number of changes that I had been recommending for years. For example, withholding was expanded to include interest and dividend payments. I started recommending that in 1959; we finally got it in 1982, but then it was reversed in 1983. I have to take the long view about seeing my tax policy recommendations realized. But I think my general ideas about tax erosion, about comprehensive income taxation, have percolated through to the public and policy-makers. I hope some of my detailed proposals will be adopted in the future.

There are a number of ways in which my ideas influence tax policy. Some of the key people in the tax legislative process come to me at Brookings—congressional committee aides, for example. They ask for copies of my articles and also solicit my advice in telephone conversations and interviews. And then there are the people who have studied or worked at Brookings in the Studies in Government Finance Program. They teach and write about taxation, and my ideas get disseminated in that way.

One mode of communication is through formal and informal discussion with people in the administrative branch of the government. Off and on I have been a consultant to the Treasury Department on tax matters. The staffs of the Treasury Department in all administrations, Republican and Democratic, have been friendly with me and communicate with me. I don't know how much this is just communication and how much influence. As for testimony in congressional hearings, the staffs seem to assume that when matters of income taxation come up, the committees should hear from me, partly because I have definite views and state them with vigor.

Incidentally, there's quite a difference between my testimony before congressional committees and my professional writings. I feel that when I write an article or book under the auspices of Brookings, I ought to be scientific, analytical, and unemotional. When I come before a committee, I put in a little jazz. I'm invited to testify because the more senior congressmen on the committees have learned that they can get straight answers from me. A lot of people waffle. Congressmen don't like that. They like definite opinions, and I have them.

I'll give my advice to anybody who wants it, and I'm pleased that prominent people have wanted it. I think my first contact with politicians occurred way back when I was an employee of the Treasury Department in the 1950s. I got to know Hubert Humphrey, who was then the junior senator from Minnesota. He used me, and of course a number of other people, for information and guidance on tax matters. We created quite a tax expert in Hubert Humphrey. As a result, throughout his political career, Hubert was a great tax reformer. I was also a friend of Paul Douglas, also a tax reformer in the Senate, and Herbert Lehman, formerly governor of New York State and then senator from that state.

I got to know such people extremely well socially as well as professionally. I was, and still am, a good friend of Stanley Surrey, who was assistant secretary of the Treasury for taxation in the Kennedy Administration. Jack Kennedy did recommend, as has practically every president since then, a comprehensive tax reform, but he got only a piece of what he wanted. I was a consultant to the Treasury Department during that time. I was heavily involved in trying to promote the Revenue Act of 1964, the big tax cut proposed by Walter Heller to promote economic expansion. During this period I also continued my contacts with people on the Hill. You have to come at tax reform through both the administration and the Congress.

Finally, I also had a direct influence on Jimmy Carter's views on taxation. He had read my book (written jointly with George Break) *Federal Tax Reform: The Impossible Dream* and was impressed by it. He told me that his interest in tax reform began with reading my book. He came to Brookings when he was still an unknown. We had lunch and he expressed a great interest in the subject. I was his tax adviser during the 1976 campaign. However, I did not join the Carter Administration largely because of the opposition of Senator Russell Long. His opposition to me was reported in several newspaper articles at the time. Long objected to my being a major influence on taxation in the Carter Administration. I've never talked to Jimmy Carter about this, but I think he decided he could not buck the powerful senator on this issue. Instead of me he appointed as assistant secretary for taxation my good friend Lawrence Woodworth, who was then chief of staff of the Joint Taxation Committee. Nonetheless, I remained a consultant to the Treasury Department and I used to see Jimmy Carter and wrote memoranda for him during his first two years in office when he was talking about tax reform. In a moment, when I speak about the kinds and sources of resistance to my ideas on income taxation, I'll say some more about why Long was opposed to me. It was nothing personal; indeed we were always friendly to one another.

Occasionally, I have tried to reach the public directly with some of my ideas. As I have already indicated, I write articles for magazines and newspapers from time to time. I was particularly active in promoting the Kennedy tax reform and tax cut proposals that eventually became the Revenue Act of 1964. I also supported the Vietnam war surtax, which President Johnson resisted for so long. I was doing so both in my capacity as a consultant to the Treasury Department and the Council of Economic Advisors and in my public capacity, in testimony to Congress. When Johnson didn't take our advice, I helped bring together about a thousand economists to pay for and sign an advertisement in the newspapers urging Johnson to balance the budget during the Vietnam war. That ad was not unlike the ad that some businessmen recently published trying to persuade President Reagan to cut the budget deficit.

Of course, I've always had some influence through teaching the junior people who have spent time with us at Brookings. And I have taught seminars on tax policy at the Georgetown Law School and the Stanford Law School. Some of my research assistants and students are now members of eminent law firms and some work either in the Treasury Department or at the Congressional Budget Office. Most of the pre-docs and the research assistants I've had at Brookings have become university professors. I tease some of my legal friends when one of my students becomes a lawyer, rather than an economist, saying that I feel I've lost someone. This is not so really, because most of them remain interested in tax policy, either as tax practitioners or as professors of tax law.

I remain an active source of information for, and an intermediary among, many people interested in taxation. I have contacts with academics across the whole political spectrum, from conservative to liberal. I'm on a friendly basis with a great many public finance professors and they use me as a sort of center for information. Many of these people were connected at one time or another with us in our program of Government Finance Studies. They are now some of the major public finance professors in the country. My intermediary role is very much enhanced by the fact that I'm in Washington where the main events connected with tax policy are going on.

The government finance program in particular and Brookings as a policy organization in general have been influential in a movement, so far not successful, to establish a "Brookings" in Europe. And I've just returned from Israel, where I was invited to join the board of the Center for Social Policy, which is trying to become the Brookings of that country.

I've already referred to some resistance to my ideas. Here's an example. Some years ago I was approached by an editor of the *Reader's Digest* who had read some of my stuff and wanted to condense one or two of my articles. I said, doubtingly, "For the *Reader's Digest?*" And he said, "Yeah, I'll bet'cha I can sell it to the editors." I said, "Well, I'll be glad to have you do it, but I doubt that you'll sell it to the *Reader's Digest*." He said, "You've got the same view of the *Reader's Digest* that a lot of other intellectuals have." Well, he prepared a digest of one of my articles, most of which I had to rewrite. We finally came to an agreement on a popularized version of what I had said. It was at least accurate, not complete but accurate. Six months later I received a small check from the *Reader's Digest* with a note from my friend saying that I was right, that the *Reader's Digest* did not want the article, but here's something for your troubles.

Some of the opposition to my ideas is intellectual, but not so much about my basic premise, the idea of comprehensive income taxation, that if you want to tax income you should tax it in full. Rather, the major intellectual difference is about the appropriateness of the income tax as a way of taxing people. They prefer another form of taxation, a sales tax or a graduated consumption tax. That has been the major source of difference.

More recently, there has emerged a group of economists who argue that we ought to promote savings and investment and who feel that our income tax system has destroyed incentives for savings and investment. So they have strayed from comprehensive income taxation to support such deductions as Keoghs and IRAs and "all-saver" certificates and things like that. I regard such deductions as pure giveaways. All they do is permit affluent people like me to reduce their taxes. They don't increase their savings one bit.

The major source of resistance to my ideas has come from special interest groups. Every group with strong interests in the present set of deductions—business groups, the aged, labor, homeowners, the medical profession, charitable organizations—sees me as an enemy. As I have already said, one of the results of my research is that the loopholes in the income tax law are not loopholes for the rich alone. There are loopholes for people throughout the whole scale of income. And so my ideas are bucking up against the interests of important groups in the community, even those that might otherwise be regarded as liberal.

I don't want to be invidious, but I might mention a few groups that oppose my views. The United States Chamber of Commerce and the National Association of Manufacturers consider my views antibusiness. Real estate dealers disagree with me because I'm against real estate tax shelters and homeowner tax preference. Labor unions disagree with me on the issue of taxing social security benefits and unemployment compensation. The banks and savings and loan associations don't like me for recommending that taxes on interest and dividends be withheld. I have been recommending that ever since I was in the Treasury Department in the early 1950s. And so for the case I mentioned earlier, Senator Russell Long's opposition, that's pretty much based on differences in values. We're friendly enough with one another; he knows my views well. Occasionally, we even agree. But he thinks that I'm just too liberal, that I want to soak the rich, which is not the case. On principle, he wants less progressivity in income taxation than I do, and then, on specifics, he also tends to protect particular interests.

Now I want to draw some general inferences from a long career as an economist and researcher. Since I've spent most of my professional life in an academic research environment, I feel strongly that research *is* helpful to the political system and to people and opinion leaders in making up their minds about social and economic policies. A social scientist has the responsibility to develop concepts, ideas, and measurements that will produce nonpartisan, unbiased analysis. I think that Brookings does an excellent job in this field. That is a major tenet of my whole life, that social scientists can be useful in helping to promote improvements in public policy. It's not only my own experience that validates this view, but the experience of the Brookings Institution as a whole. I've been working here for more than twenty years, and a lot of the work that we've done has had important policy results. For example, the whole idea of a congressional budget was developed at the Brookings Institution; the person who helped develop it was Alice Rivlin, who was the first director of the Congressional Budget Office.

My experience has also taught me that there are groups with economic and political power who can exercise their influence to prevent what I would regard as improvements in social policy. It's unfortunate, I think, that there are such centers of power to prevent progress. But I suppose that one shouldn't expect anything else. When you change social policy, some people gain and some people lose. It's a value-judgment as to whether the trade-off is worth it. There are some economists who argue that the status quo is the best place to be, because if you change the status quo you're going to generate too many windfall losses. That's one of the reasons why deregulation is so difficult.

When you try to change policy, people who have economic advantages that would be eroded oppose the change. Taxation is another area in which some people stand to lose from a change, while others stand to gain. And when you talk about something as big as comprehensive income taxation, you are really entering the lion's den with a great many powerful interests.

Sometimes I'm pessimistic about social change, but on the whole I have a sort of upbeat or optimistic view that in the end we do make progress, although slowly. It's a constant fight. One of the problems is that there are a lot of well-meaning people out there—politicians, government officials, and others—who want to do the right thing but don't know how to manage fiscal affairs. Basically, I'm a fiscal conservative and a liberal on social policy. A lot of businessmen are amazed to learn that Pechman is interested in balancing the budget. But the question of balancing the budget is quite neutral as to how the federal government should use its powers and responsibilities to promote the general welfare. I think that you can help the poor, have a good social security system, and defend the country and still have a balanced budget. The implementation of fiscal policy, which has been one of my major concerns, has been less than satisfactory throughout my career. As a result, economic progress has been jerky, sporadic. Then, in the 1970s we got this terrible inflation, which not only reduced the welfare of many people directly, but also eroded much of the social progress that we made in the 1960s. So, one can see that there is change, and sometimes change for the good, but it's sporadic, it's difficult, and we have to keep working for it.

For the future, as part of this work, I want to finish my research on the distribution of income. That's been one of my abiding interests ever since I wrote my Ph.D. dissertation at the University of Wisconsin. I want to prepare an analysis of the data developed at Brookings under my supervision on the distribution of income both before and after tax. I also want to pull together my essays, many of them on income taxation, but on other matters, too. And I want to do more on the negative income tax.

I have been associated with the negative income tax movement almost from its beginning in the United States. One of the great disappointments of my life is that we didn't make more progress on negative income taxation, which I think would have greatly improved our welfare system. A negative income tax is a dignified and effective method of helping the poor to live in a decent way, and to give them an opportunity to get out of poverty. It would also add a desirable degree of progressivity to our income tax system. During the 1970s, both President Nixon and President Carter were persuaded to recommend a form of negative income taxation, but both proposals made little headway in Congress. I'd like to get back to this subject again.

One shouldn't exaggerate the progress or the influence that people like me have had on tax and social policy. After all, we still have a tax system and a welfare system that need to be reformed. I think we can say that we've made some progress, but the remaining agenda is very long. That's why there's so much more work to be done.

Chapter Six

Merton J. Peck

Deregulation of the Transportation Industry

*Merton J. Peck, of the Yale University Department of Economics,
has been involved, fairly continuously from the very beginning of
his career, in the economics of transportation. The research he collaborated on with other economists played its part, without their
ever intending or expecting that it would do so, in the discussion
and activity that led to the U.S. government deregulation of air
and surface transportation in the 1970s and 1980s. This deregulation occurred through both legislative enactment and regulatory
bureau decisions. Deregulation has had especially large consequences for the air transportation industry.*

Interview: Fall 1984

I went to Oberlin College where I was much taken by one professor,
Ben Lewis, who was very much interested in government regulation and
antitrust policy. Oberlin in my day, at the end of the 1940s, was a small
college with a strong tradition of sending its students on to take Ph.D.s
in leading universities. That was not a common pattern in other colleges at that time. I had started out wanting to be a lawyer, but Lewis
encouraged me to get a Ph.D. in economics. My ideal was to teach in a
small college like Oberlin.

I went to Harvard, which at that time was the dominant place for graduate education in economics. In more recent times there hasn't been any single such dominant graduate program. Because Harvard was preeminent, my "class" of fellow graduate students was extremely interesting; they made a large impression on me and in my training.

As a graduate student, I was interested in public policy; that was my definition of economics. It came as a shock to me to discover that in graduate school economics was also applied mathematics. I managed to survive in that area, but with no great success. I would have specialized in economic history, but I lacked the languages for that. I turned to the field in economics called industrial organization, the study of markets in an applied way. This was the field of my undergraduate teacher, Ben Lewis. At that time this field focused on antitrust policy and the study of unregulated industries. Industrial organization had turned its attention somewhat away from the regulated industries to antitrust and the concentrated industries. The leading economist in that field at Harvard, and perhaps in the country, at that time was Edward S. Mason. He had a great interest in public policy. He was a Washington figure, very influential in international economic policy and national security affairs. I remember an incident in his class that was very dramatic for me. His secretary knocked at the door and said, Professor Mason, you have a telephone call. He was annoyed and said, I can't take it now. But it's the President of the United States, she said. Just tell him I'm teaching a class, Mason said, turning back to his teaching. You can imagine the impression that made on a first-year graduate student; it established part of the climate in which I did my graduate work. Economics was very much involved in policy.

I did my thesis under Mason on competition in the aluminum industry and later published a book on that subject with the Harvard University Press. My training at that time gave me the impression that the regulated industries were not very intellectually interesting. Only people in the older generation worked on that topic and the younger people felt there wasn't a great deal new to be said about regulation.

My own involvement in regulation and transportation came about, like many things, by historical accident. Toward the end of my graduate work, when I was an instructor, Harvard Professor John Kenneth Galbraith was asked by the Canadian Pacific Railroad to assemble some teams of economists to look at the Canadian economy and what the future of the Canadian Pacific was likely to be in that setting. One team studied the Canadian economy and eventually published a book on that subject. Another focused on the transportation industries: on the competition between the two railroad companies that existed in Canada and on the costs of the various alternative modes of transportation. This second team consisted of John Meyer, John Stanason, Charles Zwick, and me. Meyer was then a junior fellow at Harvard. He went on to have a very distinguished career as an economist: professor at Harvard at a very early age, director of the National Bureau of Economic Research, professor at Yale, vice chairman of the Union Pacific Holding Company, which owned the Union Pacific Railroad, a member of the board of one of the Canadian Pacific subsidiaries, and, finally, a professor back at Harvard. John Stanason had worked for the Canadian Pacific but was then a graduate student at Harvard. He returned to the Canadian Pacific and became president of one of its key subsidiaries. Charles Zwick was an instructor at Harvard. He later went to the Rand Corporation, then became director of the Bureau of the Budget under President Johnson, and now is the chairman of a bank. It was a good group and what was perhaps unusual about it, as compared to other members of our class at Harvard, was that three of us had significant nonacademic careers.

A basic problem for our team was how to determine long-run marginal railroad costs for many services. Determining incremental or marginal costs in railroad services—that is, how costs vary with changes in output—was not easy. At that time there was a big dispute about passenger traffic. We were able to make progress on this question with the use of some of the newer econometric and statistical techniques that were just then being developed and applied in economics. Meyer and Zwick were both econometricians and very much involved in the founding of the Harvard Economics Department's new Statistical Laboratory.

It might be useful if I say a little about these new analytical techniques in economics. Econometrics was a major but relatively new field at that time. There was a lot of excitement about using statistical techniques in determining demand, cost, and supply functions. Economists had drawn such functions on the blackboard for years, but they hadn't had much idea of what their actual empirical shapes were. Econometrics promised, among other things, to be able to determine quantitatively the slope of those functions. Many economists, such as Lawrence Klein, who later won the Nobel Prize, were interested in railroad costs simply because there were considerable data on railroad costs. Klein, independently, and at about the same time as we were working away, published some papers on railroad costing. Railroad costs were studied for their scientific interest by economists, even those who didn't have the slightest interest in railroads as such. The older transportation economists used an approach which wasn't at all quantitative. There was a cultural gap between the older and the newer transportation economics. For example, one of the older generation, and perhaps the most famous, was Leo Sharfman of Michigan. He was president of the American Economics Association and had written an excellent five-volume study of the Interstate Commerce Commission. He discussed every ICC policy but his work was not quantitative, the way the new work was.

In the middle of our work, I accepted a position at the University of Michigan, to succeed Sharfman as a matter of fact, and I commuted from Ann Arbor to Montreal and Cambridge where our work on the Canadian transportation industry was being done. I profited from being at Michigan because Lawrence Klein had been there and had left a good group of econometricians, from whom I could learn. But I stayed there only one year and went back to be an assistant professor at the Harvard Business School, where I rejoined Meyer and Galbraith.

One of the problems we faced in using the new statistical methodology was that to do what is called "cross-section" analysis, we needed a large number of observations of railroads. Since Canada had only two railroads, we couldn't apply the method to our Canadian data. We had to use data on U.S. railroads, reasoning that what we found in the United States would be roughly applicable to Canada. We used a sample of 144 of what the ICC called "class one" railroads. We also did the cost and competitive conditions of the United States trucking industry. We did all this work on the U.S. data only to help our Canadian study; we had a very specific applied goal in mind, to understand the future of the Canadian railroads.

When we finished our study and delivered it to the Canadian Pacific, like proper academics we were all very eager to see it published. But because it had proprietary information in it, the Canadian Pacific didn't want us to do so. That was very understandable. Fortunately, they were entirely willing to have us publish all the work we had done on the U.S. railroads. Galbraith told us not to be disappointed; he said there was going to be a lot more interest in a book on the U.S. transportation industry. He said it would take us only a couple of months, but it turned out to be something like two or three years later that we staggered out with a completed manuscript on the United States, with not a word in it about Canada. We took all this time because we had become more ambitious and dealt not only with railroad costing and competition but also with the whole nature of competition between the different transportation industries in the United States. We had a lot on trucking. We also did something on the airlines, pipelines, and inland water transportation. We now had *all* the transportation industries. We even put in a little historical material.

Our book had several innovations. First of all, contrary to previous work, it was thoroughly quantitative. Second, my early training and work had been on unregulated industries with the question: suppose these were unregulated industries, how would they behave? Finally, we considered all the transportation industries in one study, in one book, as if they competed vigorously.

We closed our book with a chapter entitled "Towards Improved Transportation Policies." Our basic message was that we should move to a cost-orientated pricing system for transportation. We thought we were being very bold in saying that under such a system the underlying rationale for the regulation of the transportation system would be eliminated. Our book didn't call for a total deregulation of transportation. We weren't that bold; such boldness was to come from economists and others only later. We called only for a substantial reduction in regulation.

We might have been bolder, if we had really believed the essential point, as Galbraith was emphasizing, that technological advance had created new and very effective competitors for rail transportation. Indeed, we had dealt a lot in our book with the rise of the trucking industry and its influence on transportation. But we went some way toward recommending deregulation. We said in our last chapter that in a real sense the American experience with transportation regulation stands as an eloquent but negative test of the great strength of free enterprise, its ability to adapt quickly and efficiently to changes in the economic environment. We said that regulation constantly hindered this adaptive ability of free enterprise. We ended with a somewhat pretentious sentence: "The economic absurdities resulting from regulation of the transportation industry cried out that some action should, at long last, be taken."

The book certainly achieved its primary purpose, helping the academic reputation of its authors. Much to our surprise, and especially for a Harvard University Press academic monograph, it sold very well, going through four printings. It sold primarily to libraries and academic economists and was quite commonly used as a reading for economics courses. But it also had nonacademic influence, among officials in government agencies, railroad managers, and, to our surprise, lawyers who represented railroads or who were involved in transportation affairs. The railroad industry was beginning to have substantial financial troubles. Thus, it was a time of change and ferment when our book came out in 1959.

The biggest initial impact of our book and its findings and recommendations was on the question of rail passenger cost. Railroads said that it was extremely burdensome to run a rail passenger system, and our book supported their position. In the late stages of completing our book we had worked on the rail costing material with the support of the American Railroad Association. They were not interested in our general policy; they were very dubious about deregulation at that time, but they were very much interested in rail costs. Meyer and I, with a colleague named Gerald Kraft, published a study called "The Avoidable Costs of Rail Passenger Traffic." In sum, there was no general and strong interest in deregulation at this time. The effect of our book at that time was only on methods for determining railroad costs.

From this time forward—that is, into the 1960s and 1970s—while economic research on regulation and deregulation of the transportation industry continued, it begins to interact with a whole series of other legal, political, and social factors to produce the deregulation that eventually occurred partly by administrative action and partly by direct legislation. For example, as early as 1961, soon after he was inaugurated, President Kennedy asked James M. Landis, former dean of the Harvard Law School and an expert on administrative law and practice, to review the effectiveness of the government's administrative agencies. Although Landis did not refer in his report to our study, he concluded that there was excessive regulation by the administrative agencies. A key person in this context was the economist Kermit Gordon, then a member of Kennedy's Council of Economic Advisors. His advice influenced the Transportation Message that President Kennedy submitted to Congress in 1962. The message called for substantial deregulation of transportation, but it didn't get very far in Congress.

Continuing with the story of economic research for a moment, however: in the early 1960s, when I was invited to give a lecture at the University of Virginia, I decided to focus on the problem of the cost to society of the existing transportation regulations policies. In this lecture, I ventured an estimate of that cost. It was not a very good estimate, but subsequently making estimates of the welfare costs of regulation became a minor industry among economists. All these estimates showed that transportation regulation was very burdensome to the economy.

In the 1960s, an economist named Ann Friedlander, presently chair of the MIT Economics Department, became interested in the problems of the transportation industry. In her thesis she inquired into the costs that the trucking industry added to the construction and maintenance of highways and whether these costs were covered by the taxes paid by the trucking industry. After graduate school, she accepted a job at the

Brookings Institution, which had been interested in transportation problems for some time. Indeed, they had just sponsored a book on the railroads by James C. Nelson. Friedlander wrote a fine book, published in
1969, which supplanted our book as the standard reference on the
problems of railroads. Her book was much like ours, using what were
now the standard techniques of analysis, but it was altogether a better
job than ours.

In the middle 1960s also, because the railroads were becoming more
and more of a problem industry, the Council of Economic Advisors began to pay more attention to them. In its annual report to the President,
the council devoted a few pages to the problem of transportation regulation. It was very cautiously phrased, but it does say that, given the rise
of trucking, it would seem to be desirable to increase the role of competition and reduce the scope of government regulation over transportation rates, particularly minimum rates. In 1966 the council's report
paid even more attention to transportation, giving it six pages and a
subhead to emphasize its importance.

The key person on the council staff at this time with regard to transportation was Paul MacAvoy, who wrote those six pages; I served as
consultant to him. MacAvoy had taken his Ph.D. at Yale with a thesis on
competition in the natural gas industry. In that thesis and in the book
that came out of it, he argued a case for partial deregulation. So this
makes him one of the early deregulators.

Because we used my Virginia lecture welfare estimate of the costs of
transportation regulation in the 1966 report, we were challenged by the
trucking industry. We had to admit it was heavily based on guessing.
Nevertheless, the council had now institutionalized its position in favor
of transportation deregulation.

An economist whose work was particularly important at this time in
getting lawyers interested in deregulation was Professor Richard Caves
of Harvard. Caves had worked on the Canadian economy part of the
Canadian Pacific project. He wrote a book on airline deregulation which
is much quoted. In addition, through an economist, he wrote a book
which won a national award for being the best book in the field of administrative law. The book attracted a lot of attention and was used in
the law schools. It argued the case for airline deregulation and because
it didn't include all the technical materials on problems of costing, it
was much more accessible to lawyers. The lawyers were to be very important in deregulation later on.

For example, an article in the late 1960s by a group of Yale Law
School students in the *Yale Law Journal* was very influential probably

because its message was so clear and simple. It could be read by the noneconomists on congressional staffs and by congressmen themselves. Instead of using technical econometrical analysis in their article, these students simply compared the per mile costs of the nonregulated *intrastate* airline fares in California with the per mile regulated fares of *interstate* airline transportation. California had long hauls but no regulation so it had intensive competition and much lower fares than those between states, which were regulated by the Civil Aeronautics Board. Anyone could compare the cheaper fares of going from San Francisco to Los Angeles with the higher fares of going an equal distance, from Washington to Boston. Such dramatic examples were more credible than our complicated econometric data. Airline costs are very sensitive to the load factor, that is, the percentage of seats occupied by paying passengers. The lack of regulation in California led to more competition and lower fares, and thus to high load factors, and then in turn to low costs. Those relationships are the basis of the People's Express type of operation, which several airlines are now using.

As a sidelight, it's interesting to note that one of the Yale Law School authors was Michael Levine, who later became executive director of the CAB under the economist Alfred Kahn in the Carter Administration. Both of them were very effective deregulators through administrative action.

In Washington, the council was soon not alone in its promotion of deregulation. In the Department of Transportation, James Rodney Nelson, who was on leave from his position as a professor of economics at Amherst, was director of economic research and was in favor of deregulation. My former colleague, John Meyer, was for a while the chair of the Department of Transportation's economic research advisory committee. I, too, was on it for a while. The economists in favor of deregulation began to appear in all the relevant government agencies. John Meyer's students did work on transportation under his supervision at Harvard and then went to work at the council or in the Department of Transportation. I myself became a member of the Council of Economic Advisors in the late years of the Johnson Administration. It was becoming academic orthodoxy that there should be deregulation. There was no one who was under fifty and actively doing research in the transportation field who wasn't for deregulation.

Economists tend to believe strongly in the value of efficiency and here was a case where greater economic efficiency could be achieved. Of course, the value of equity was a constraint as to how far we could push efficiency, but we generally pushed the equity argument away or said we could show that equity goals could be achieved more cheaply by subsidy to the injured party. We were basically concerned with how to carry out the transportation functions in the economy at minimum cost in real resources. There were two equity problems, neither one trivial. One was service to the smaller communities, but we answered that, in case of railroad abandonment, trucks would serve such communities more cheaply. In the case of airlines, commuter airlines could give small cities cheaper and better service. The second equity issue was the effect of deregulation on union wages. Most of us underestimated that consequence. Regulation created monopoly profits, of which the unions took a large part. Deregulation has caused some relative decrease in the wages of truck drivers and airline pilots. On the equity issue, also, individual owners of trucks were hurt by deregulation, and so, too, were the owners of route franchises, which had been a kind of monopoly and therefore valuable, but which now lost their value under deregulation and could no longer be sold at good prices.

Still, the overriding value was efficiency. That's not as controversial a value as equity and justice. It seemed to be possible to carry on the discussion of the deregulation of the transportation industry largely in terms of the efficiency value. The main opponents of deregulation—and even some of them changed their position after a while—were the interested parties, that is, the regulated, protected industries. The protected industries were seen by most analysts, and then office-holders, and finally the public, as narrowly self-interested. The inefficiencies of regulation were so dramatic, made so clear and simple by such material as the facts on the lower fares for intrastate traffic in California as against interstate traffic elsewhere in the country, that they lent themselves to wide publicity in congressional hearings. Ordinary people and their representatives in Congress could see the inefficiency.

The Brookings Institution has been very important as a sponsor of research on deregulation. I have already mentioned that Ann Friedlander was there. In 1969, they were awarded a large grant from the Ford Foundation for their program of studies on regulation. When I left the government at the end of the Johnson Administration, I went to Brookings to be in that program. I was succeeded there by Roger Noll, who had worked at the council on transportation problems. Noll is a very able economist and a person of great energy. He was interested in the question of what kind of regulation made sense. When he later went back to Cal Tech as professor, he trained students who continued his kind of work. Noll was followed at Brookings by Theodore Keeler, on leave from Berkeley, whose book *Railroads, Freight, and Public Policy* is like our book and Friedlander's, but better than both. It is now the standard text. There has been a real progression of economic research and analysis in this field. Keeler's book is in the Brookings series on the regulation of economic activity, which was supported by the Ford grant. Noll has a book in that series, too. Altogether there are about fifteen to twenty books in it; you can see that we had a kind of industry in this field. We began to spread out from transportation to other regulated fields. Noll, McGowen, and I did a book on television. Interest spread into all kinds of telecommunications and into safety and health problems. More recently, the American Enterprise Institute has started a journal on this topic, *Regulation*. Paul MacAvoy was involved in the establishment of that journal.

The general case for deregulation was very much helped along by research that was being done in the early 1970s on the effects of regulation on airline fares. I have already mentioned the early work by Caves and the article by the students at the Yale Law School. These early works were taken into account in a major investigation of domestic passenger fares that was undertaken by the CAB in 1970–71. Even more important for this investigation was a book by the Canadian economist William A. Jordan, *Airlines Regulation in America: Effects and Imperfections* (1971). It had a lot of new material in it. Critical material was also presented in the CAB investigation by two economists from the Department of Transportation, George Douglas and James C. Miller III. They had succeeded Nelson in the economics research section of the department. Douglas and Miller later wrote up their material for still another book in the Brookings series; its title is *Economic Regulation of Domestic Air Transportation: Theory and Policy*. I would say it is an advance over Caves, Jordan, and others. It showed that the CAB regulatory methods had huge inherent flaws because essentially it is a cost-plus system. They pointed out that under this fixed-fare and cost-plus system, airlines could compete only by having more flights, better service, and better amenities. All these drive up costs and become the basis for higher fixed fares. These higher fares reduce the load factor, still further driving up costs. Thus, following the CAB's methods of fare regulation, you ultimately get a situation that was well captured by the humorist Art Buchwald, who had either read the Douglas and Miller material or heard about it from Washington cocktail party talk. Buchwald wrote a piece in which he described airline fares as rising continually and so high that eventually only such fabulously wealthy individuals as J. Paul Getty and the Shah of Iran could afford them. Finally, according to Buchwald, Getty calls up the Shah and says even he can no longer afford the fares and so they will have to be doubled for the Shah. Buchwald has several clever articles that seem to be straight out of economics journals, but without all the equations. That is one of the ways our new research and analysis gets into public opinion, or at least attracts an attentive public.

An important political event for the antiregulatory movement was some hearings held by Senator Kennedy in the middle 1970s. I don't know how he got interested, but Senator Kennedy was chairman of the Administrative Practices Sub-Committee of the Senate Judiciary Committee and, since everything in the government involves administrative practices, his committee had a license to look at a lot of things. Kennedy became interested in deregulation and hired Steven Breyer as counsel and organizer of the hearings. Breyer, then a Harvard law professor, is now a federal judge. He had been very much influenced by the work of economists and had done two important studies in the field of regulation. One was a book with Paul MacAvoy on natural gas regulation; through Paul he came to know all of the economic literature. He was really a member of the community. He and MacAvoy published, under the auspices of the Brookings Institution, *Energy Regulation by the Federal Power Commission*. For the hearings, Kennedy and Breyer decided to focus on airline regulation. Breyer had a very good staff of smart young lawyers. They were able to show that some of the airline presentations were extremely flawed. I testified and so did other economists like Roger Noll and Jim Miller.

The movement for deregulation of the transportation industry culminated in effective administrative and legislative actions in the late 1970s and the early 1980s. In the case of the airlines, it resulted in total deregulation: the Civil Aeronautics Board, as the result of a 1978 legislative act, went out of existence on December 31, 1984. In the case of the railroads and trucking industry, deregulation has been considerable but not complete. The ICC still exists. Deregulation has followed somewhat different patterns for the different transportation industries.

The story of railroad and trucking deregulation is more complicated than that of the airlines. The railroads had been financially ailing for a long time, but the real crisis came in 1970 when the Penn Central Railroad went into bankruptcy. That event, widely reported in the general press, made it apparent to everyone in what bad shape the railroads were. In the Nixon Administration, the Council of Economic Advisors set up a commission under John Meyer to study railroad productivity and other problems. His report was quite influential.

There was a lot of different legislation concerning railroads and trucking. There was a Con Rail Act and the creation of the U.S. Railroad Association, which was to reorganize the northeast railroads. In 1970, on the initiative of the Interstate Commerce Commission, the so-called 3-R Act was passed. That gave railroad rate-making freedom to the railroads. The trouble was, according to the advocates of deregulation, that the ICC still interpreted the act in such a way as not to give the railroads full freedom. In 1976, the so-called 4-R Act (the Railroad Revitalization and Regulatory Reform Act) was passed; it was still more deregulatory than the 3-R Act. As it had in the case of the CAB, the Carter Administration appointed to the ICC chairmanship a strong deregulator in the person of the economist Darius Gaskins. Carter also appointed another economist, Marcus Alexsis. The ICC began deregulating administratively, just as the CAB did under Kahn. However, there remained more tension in the ICC over deregulation of railroads and trucking. One of the reasons for that is the strong political influence of the Teamsters Union. The Staggers Rail Act of 1980 is now the controlling legislation for the ICC, and while it is more liberal than earlier legislation on deregulation, it still does not prescribe the elimination of the ICC and there remains more regulation than for airlines.

In sum, what started in empirical economic research and was advanced by its convergence with a variety of other research and a variety of social factors has resulted finally in considerable deregulation of the transportation industries. Much has been done; perhaps more remains to be done. Many of the same economists and other actors were involved all along. Indeed, in some of the newer deregulatory areas, such as telecommunications and energy, the same people show up. For example, Paul MacAvoy has continued active on energy deregulation as has Roger Noll on telecommunications. And lawyers who were active are now on the federal bench, with its power to affect regulation. Breyer was appointed to the federal bench by Carter, and Richard Posner, a Chicagoan who was active in the Johnson Administration in telecommunications regulation, has now been appointed to the federal court of appeals by President Reagan.

I have said that much has been done for competition as a result of deregulation. Here are a few illustrative figures: as of 1982, there were more than 70 airlines regularly serving passengers in this country, as compared to 33 such airlines before deregulation. Among these 70 are a dozen who offer interstate service, several of whom now operate in such heavily traveled routes as the Northeast Corridor at fares considerably below those of the older established airlines. In trucking, some 22,000 carriers are now licensed to operate, as against about 15,000 before deregulation. Almost 8,000 carriers entered the trucking industry between July 1980 and May 1982. This is what deregulation and competition have created in the transportation industry. It has been at the cost of the monopoly profits of the formerly regulated industries and of the high wages of unionized employees, but it has resulted in greater overall productivity and increased public welfare. Fifty years of regulation were now all but at an end. What none of us expected in the early 1950s, when we started our research, had actually happened.

In conclusion, and by way of summing up, through some general views of what I've learned from my long involvement in and observation of the area of transportation industry deregulation, I am struck by three propositions about the relations between economic research and social policy. First, you need a substantial body of research to be mined by policy-makers. I am skeptical of the one dramatic book that makes a difference. An apparent counter-example is Keynes' *General Theory,* but even that work would have gone nowhere in the policy world without a whole set of subsidiary writings, research, and modifications. The deregulation story is not the story of one book or one person but of a small social movement, consisting of a set of people who interacted face to face and who took a common view of the problem. Of course, like all academics, they were not without their squabbles, but on the whole it was a remarkable consensus.

Second, the people who knew the research backwards and forwards believed in it strongly and were willing to interact with people whose main role was that of political activist. The researchers, as we have seen, got directly involved in the policy-making process. Third, the research would probably have had little impact had there not been the several social forces we have described to sweep it along. There was big trouble in the railroad industry, there was the consumer movement, there was the recession, there was criticism of the regulatory agencies as being too much in the power of the regulated industries, and there were members of Congress and their staffs looking for viable issues. All of this came together in the 1970s. If our research had been carried out, let us say, from 1920 to 1925, a very prosperous period for the railroads, it would have had little impact. You need the sense that there is a problem; people just don't believe that much in academic research. But once there is a generally defined sense of a social problem, then policy-makers will look to the economic research.

All of this indicates that it's not easy to predict social change. At the very beginning of the 1970s, we had a conference at the Brookings Institution in which the transportation industry researchers concluded that we would probably be coming to the same conference ten years hence, with no change having occurred. We were all persuaded that there was a kind of social immobilism that prevented solutions for increasing efficiency in transportation from being accepted. All solutions were going to break someone's rice bowl. We felt all the political power rested with the producers and that therefore no change would occur. But within five years there was a dramatic change for all the reasons and from all the forces I've mentioned above. We didn't calculate the effectiveness of what I might call the "policy entrepreneurs," the policy activists who brought together these many social forces with our economic research about the policy value of effective competition in the transportation industry. I have a feeling of amazement at all that has occurred. There has been more of a difference than I ever thought possible. Not everything that everyone wanted has happened but a lot has in this pretty pluralist world of ours.

Unemployment Insurance Payments and Recidivism Among Released Prisoners

*Peter Rossi, of the University of Massachusetts, Amherst, has been
an active and continuous empirical social researcher on social
policy questions for more than thirty years. This is because, as he
says, he is interested in solving social policy "puzzles" or, better,
contributing something to their solution. In the case he describes
here, a randomized field experiment of the effects of unemployment
insurance payments on recidivism among released prisoners in
Georgia and Texas, we find a mixture of actual policy effects and
a failure to achieve such effects for interesting political and administrative reasons. This partly "negative" case highlights some of
the ways in which policy effects are successfully achieved.*

Interview: June 1983

I really began by being interested in applied work. As an undergraduate I wanted to become a social worker, and it may be that I
finally didn't get into that field because so many other opportunities
opened up after World War II. I got into graduate school to study
sociology, thinking that I'd take at least an M.A. and see how it would
go. I went to Columbia mainly because that was the only place that
would admit me, given my undergraduate record. Those were the days,

just after World War II, when it was said that, at Columbia, sociological theory and research were being brought together in a new, closer way by Robert Merton and Paul Lazarsfeld, the former being the theorist, the latter the researcher. I first tried working with Merton, but that didn't come off. I was doing an M.A. thesis with him, but every time we met he seemed to have some new ideas for me to try. The damn thesis was getting to be my life's work, so I decided to bypass it and go for the Ph.D. and do a different thesis for that.

Paul Lazarsfeld had different interests and standards from Merton. He had enthusiasms, sometimes randomly capricious and arbitrary. I wrote a course paper for him which involved some data analysis and one of those random fits of enthusiasm came over him. He invited me to join the staff at the Bureau of Applied Social Research and work with him and on the various empirical social researches that were being carried out there. From that point on it did turn out that I had some kind of aptitude for empirical work and particularly for quantitative analysis. So Paul's influence upon my work, at least in the early period, was very, very strong. This was a methodological influence, not a substantive one. On my own, later, I worked on a variety of problems in urban sociology, social stratification, and political sociology. Nearly from the beginning of my career, there really hasn't been much plan or strong direction to my work. It's opportunistic in character, as I see it. That is to say, the opportunity would arise to do a fairly good piece of work, and what dominated my decision to do it or not was not the substantive character of the work but the puzzle that it presented. The puzzle was an intellectual puzzle, how to understand this particular phenomenon given the apparatus of contemporary empirical research. For example, once I was faced with the problem of why some universities and colleges produce a higher quality of product in the way of students than do others. Is it because they get better students and it doesn't matter what the school does, or does the school add some special character to a person's career? That's a puzzle. I wasn't particularly interested in higher education, but the puzzle consisted in trying to untangle the web of relationships that exist between the demographic composition of a student body and the activities of the school in terms of its curriculum and instructors. I've gone from intellectual puzzle to intellectual puzzle. The study I'm going to describe here, of recidivism among released prisoners, was a puzzle for me. I didn't do the original design of the study. I was called in after a third of the data had already been collected. When the Department of Labor sponsors of the study realized they had a puzzle on their hands that they couldn't solve, given the people who had designed the study and who were going to do the analysis of the data, they called me in. They called in the study doctor; that's me.

The puzzles that I'm interested in usually have both theoretical and methodological aspects to them. The intellectual framework and the methodology make it possible to interpret the puzzle. I don't come to these puzzles with any fixed or stable set of ideas; I take my theory and methodology where I can find them. Columbia didn't train me into any particular theory or methodology. In fact, although there was a lot of talk about bringing theory and methodology together there, I didn't find it that way. It seemed to me that Merton was more concerned to find an explanation than to test it. And as for Paul Lazarsfeld, he was perfectly content with any explanation that would work. He wasn't concerned with the integration of that explanation with any other body of material.

There certainly wasn't any theoretical purpose behind the recidivism study. The study was devised to test a Department of Labor program to see whether providing unemployment insurance benefits to released prisoners would help them to reform their behavior. It was a very specific program coming out of a very specific mandate given to the Department of Labor under the Employment Training Act of 1964. It was quite divorced from both a very relevant part of microeconomic theory and an equally relevant body of sociological theory on employment and work. Despite the fact that the people who were sponsoring the research and designing it, together with an advisory group of distinction, included labor economists and sociologists, there doesn't seem to be any evidence in the early documentation of this study of what one would ordinarily expect in the way of explicit theory. I think this is typical of certain narrow types of applied research where what predominates are a concern for a program and the ad hoc hope that the program will work and a desire to have some kind of evidence that it will or won't work. The general stance is optimistic and hopeful, hoping that this time we'll hit upon something that works. It's Edisonian in character: well, this material is not going to produce the necessary filament for the electric bulb, so let's try something else; tungsten looks like bamboo, so let's try bamboo. The Department of Labor program kept on trying. One of the consequences of this kind of approach is that they don't learn from experience. They do the same things over again. When a new regime comes in, there develops the notion that the program will actually work this time when we do it right. I've been around long enough now to see different regimes going over the same track on this and other programs. For example, the different administrations keep on resurrecting manpower training programs despite the inefficiency of

such programs in producing results and despite the tremendous cost
per measurable effect.

On the methodological side, there was something new and interesting about the study. At that time, there had developed a great deal of
interest in using randomized controlled experiments for large-scale social research with policy consequence. It was fashionable to do controlled experiments. It was as if the sponsors of this study had said,
everybody else is using controlled experiments these days, we should,
too. More recently, we've had a similar methodological fashion of doing
longitudinal studies, which are built on the idea that in order to untangle cause and effect in some behavior we have to study people over
a long period of time. The behavioral processes are thought to take a
long period of time and so we need longitudinal studies that cover the
same period of time. But in the late 1960s and early 1970s controlled
experiments were all the thing; the best known example is the negative
income tax experiments.

The controlled experiment methodology of the study appealed to me.
I had written a volume for the Russell Sage Foundation on the evaluation of the first income maintenance experiment and criticized it. But I
always felt uncomfortable just being a critic. I have always felt that a
good critic has to be someone who can speak from the knowledge and
authority of having himself done what he or she is criticizing. So as
soon as Howard Rosen, the program officer responsible for the study in
the Department of Labor, approached me about doing the analysis of
the study, I said, this is my opportunity. I can now say that I have had a
hand, if not in the original design of the study, at least in its analysis.
I would be able to speak with more authority than previously about
large-scale social experiments. Professor Hans Zeisel, who was on the
advisory committee and who came to differ with me later on about my
analysis, has, I think, overestimated how good the experiment is. On the
surface, at least, it looks good. It certainly was better conducted in the
sense that there are fewer holes in the data than in some of the other
studies that were done at about the same time. We had much less attri-
tion of our subjects. In terms of its general design, the study was carried out very well, but what Zeisel does not appreciate is how bad the
data are. The data were collected by amateurs and when you touch the
data in any direct way, the flaws and the enormous amount of measurement error in the study become immediately apparent. I know Zeisel
did not work with the data in any intimate way. There are a lot of miss-
ing data in the interviews, seemingly arbitrary gaps. There didn't seem
to be, when I first looked at the data closely, any particular reason why

an interviewer didn't get the proper measures of what the interviewee had done during the past three months. The interviewers got the interviews; that's what shows on the surface, an 85 percent response rate overall. But when I met the interviewers, I began to know what the trouble was. Those in Texas, for example, were detached prison guards. When I asked the head of the prison system in Texas how he picked those guards to be interviewers, he replied, "Well, we really didn't know what to do with them, so we sent them out on this detached service." Because of the high response rate, some of my collaborators have suggested that these not too highly motivated amateurs were good at tracking down the released prisoners. But others, more cynical perhaps, think that they made up some of the interviews. I don't know what to believe.

In addition to the puzzle and methodological features of the study, the values that lay behind it were also attractive to me. The general value system of the middle-class liberal is very much behind government programs to help disadvantaged workers of which this study was a part. What the program says is that the released prisoners are disadvantaged people and that a small amount of advantage given to them by these unemployment compensation dollars can be multiplied into a very big advantage for both them and the society. It assumes that if the society puts people in circumstances where they have no income and have no skills, then they will steal. It further assumes that if these people have a sufficient amount of support, their true colors will shine through. And they will stop thievery and go to work. And I believe that. I laugh at my acceptance of these assumptions because there isn't very much empirical evidence to support them. That's my value stance toward the world. We even jokingly suggested that we title the book which reported the study *Doing Good to the Bad*. Those are the values behind the study. There are some kinds of research I wouldn't do because I reject the program and policy behind it on value grounds. For example, if this had been a study on how to detect the hardened criminal so that society could put him away forever, it's something I would not have done. I reject the policy of incarcerating people even if and just because it lowered the crime rate; I reject it on value grounds.

This study, I should explain, was the successor to the so-called LIFE (Living Insurance For Ex Felons) experiment in Baltimore. I'll say more about that earlier study in a little while. Whereas that study seemed to have produced the effect desired, that is, a reduction of recidivism, the study I got involved in seemed to be failing, that is, not producing any effects whatsoever. Or even worse, and this is what drove the sponsors up the wall, it looked for a while as if there might even be perverse effects, that is, the experimental or test group was actually committing more crime than those not getting the unemployment compensation. That's when Rosen called me in to be the study doctor, that's when these puzzle, methodological, and value features all came together simultaneously to make me agree to complete the study. I didn't begin my participation with any single purpose but with all of these together.

Practically all of the funding for this study came from the federal government, of course. There were two different sources in the government. The Law Enforcement Assistance Administration contributed about a third of the financing, although eventually they lost interest in the study. The other two thirds came from the Department of Labor. Howard Rosen, the main force behind the study, was a master at putting together various pieces of money necessary for a study. In the Department of Labor, the funds came partly from CETA (Comprehensive Employment and Training Administration) money and partly from Rosen's own research funds. Rosen was a trained labor economist, research director for the Department of Labor's manpower training and employment division. He had been directing research programs in the department for at least twenty years; he was one of the old mules. In addition to the federal funds, there were small amounts of state funds involved in the form of donated labor. In Texas and Georgia, employees were detailed from the employment security agencies of those two states and also there were the prison employees that I've mentioned. But, essentially, the funds and resources were coming from the federal government.

Given the apparent success of the earlier experiment on which our experiment was building, the LIFE experiment in Baltimore, it was expected that there would be some positive effect of the payments we were making to the released prisoners upon their recidivism and that the effect would be large enough so that it would be cost-effective to use this program as a means of significantly reducing crime and its associated costs. At first glance, however, using traditional analysis of variance techniques, it looked as if the experiment in both states, Georgia and Texas, was having no effects. This was an enormous disappointment to Howard Rosen and his colleagues. Part of the mandate which was given to me when I joined the project half way through was to see whether these initial negative or null findings were in fact the case or whether there was some kind of complicated masking phenomenon going on in which the effects produced in Baltimore were being masked by some other effects such as from the different administration of the experiment. The Baltimore experiment, which had been run by the sociologist Ken Lenihan, who was very much committed to the program and its success, may have been different in significant ways from its administration by the employment security and prison bureaucracies in Georgia and Texas.

The initial negative findings made it look as if an enormous program apparatus, supported by something on the order of $3 million, was going down the drain. There were also political elements involved that were not going to be realized because of the negative findings. The American Bar Association had committed itself to be the political front-runner for the new experiment. They received a very large sum of money from the Department of Labor to monitor the experiment (and to prepare the legislation that would come out of it). They hired Ken Lenihan from the Baltimore predecessor study to do the monitoring for them. ABA was doing the legal research on the employment security system to justify the legislation that would enable the states to pay unemployment benefits to the released prisoners. All the background papers had been prepared and work had been done by the American Bar Foundation's Commission on Criminal Law. If the experiment had shown clear and positive effects, the Bar Association was going to carry out the lobbying in Congress. They had identified the various members of Congress who would be supportive of the new legislation on the appropriate committees and had even arranged to have a TV show with interviews with released prisoners who would have testified that it was the payments that had made the difference in their not committing further crimes. A whole apparatus was in place for a major push for change in the existing federal legislation.

But by the time I came into the study, it was quite clear that this apparatus could not be used. Not unless I managed to find some definite positive effects, that is, something convincing. The whole effort came to a halt and nothing has ever come of it. I could never explain to the people at the American Bar Association what I finally did find. It was apparently too complicated an analysis for them to either use or understand. Indeed, I never quite convinced Howard Rosen and I certainly was never able to convince Hans Zeisel from our advisory board.

In doing my analysis, I went back first to the Baltimore study to see what had occurred there to cause the positive effect that they got. There were several possibilities. First, the Baltimore experiment could have been the one study in twenty that by chance produces an effect; that is always a possibility. Another was that Ken Lenihan was doing something in Baltimore that the states of Georgia and Texas could not reproduce. I mean the tender loving care with which he handled those released prisoners in Maryland simply could not be delivered by a large-scale state agency. The third possibility was that something that was unanticipated in the design of the experiment surfaced and that we had found something that hadn't appeared in Baltimore at all. I noticed in the data that the people in the experimental group, the test group, those getting the payments, had worked considerably less over the course of the year in which they were followed. That suggested to me that the payments, the experimental treatment, was actually providing a very strong work disincentive. I remembered from having looked at the income maintenance experiments that there, too, was controversy over whether the money payments were or were not a work disincentive. I felt that the microeconomic theory about trade-offs between work and leisure might be relevant. Accordingly, we did some homework on the workers' incentive literature. As a result, we had to ask ourselves, if these payments do act as they are said to in classical microeconomic theory, that is, dissuade people from working, then why didn't that effect occur in Baltimore?

A rather simple answer came up, one that we didn't talk about much in our book. In questioning Lenihan closely, we found that he had not administered the experiment according to the design plan. The plan was that released prisoners in Baltimore were to be given the unemployment insurance benefits only if they were not working. Lenihan thought that was cruel. So he just wrote the checks and delivered them whether the subjects were working or not. He felt that if they were working steadily for three or four months, they would by that time have exhausted their benefits. They felt he had fulfilled the spirit of the plan, if not the letter. Under these circumstances, no disincentives to the desired effect appeared.

Another thing we looked at is the meaning of work and why it provides a disincentive for engaging in crime. It's partly because work provides an alternative source of income. There's competition between work and crime as sources of income. We tried to find some data on what the typical returns are from the type of crimes our subjects engaged in, but we couldn't find anything. The experts were reluctant to make guesses, but when they did, they made guesses around $100 a week, but even that was said to be very irregular and erratic. That is somewhat lower than they would have made on the average if they worked in the kind of job they would get in Georgia and Texas. So the income competition between illegal crime and legal work was something that microeconomic theory showed us we should consider.

There was a further consideration in the nature of work. Doing illegal activities takes time, and so does work. If one works, one has less time to commit crimes. Furthermore, working provides the worker with status, a disincentive for crime, a source of social support for going straight.

So finally putting all these ideas from microeconomic and sociological theory together, I came up with the view that what was going on was a kind of masking effect in which the treatments were providing both a work disincentive and a crime disincentive. The crime disincentive occurred because the released prisoners felt it wasn't worthwhile to engage in crime, if by doing nothing they could get seventy or eighty bucks a week. The work disincentive operates in much the same way but in the opposite direction. I decided that we were dealing with *counterbalancing social processes*. When it comes to individual motivation, we don't think in this way, in terms of counterbalancing forces. Counterbalancing social processes is not easy either to demonstrate empirically or to communicate verbally to people who don't think in those terms. That's why we had such difficulty, and didn't succeed, in convincing the Bar Association people and Howard Rosen that this was a reasonable analysis of our data.

The trick now for policy was how to give away the money without using the no work rule of the unemployment security system and thus recapture the kinds of effects which Lenihan got in Baltimore. And it also became increasingly clear that Lenihan had used some very special incentives and methods in Baltimore. For example, once when I was visiting him in his office—I was teaching at Johns Hopkins then—an office he had set up in a storefront from which he administered the project and dispensed the payment checks, he suddenly looked out the window, jumped up from his seat, and ran outside to remonstrate with two very large black fellows who were out there. When he came back in he explained that the two fellows were fighting and that one of them was part of the experimental group. He had gone out to keep the fellows from getting into trouble. He was always dispensing a lot of TLC. When one of his subjects got a job, he would advance him money to buy work clothes or tools or whatever he needed to go to work. He'd even show up at his subjects' doorsteps with his car to take them to work the first few days to get them used to how to get there. Thus, there was a lot going on that wasn't in the plan.

I came to think that the best we could do was to give the money to the released prisoners as an entitlement, not making it conditional upon their being unemployed. Presumably the best way of doing this would be to get the payments to people only in the situation where they had tried getting work but failed. This then would be a reward for having tried, and unfortunately also for having failed. That's presumably the way in which the unemployment benefit system should work but apparently it does not. So we came up with the notion that released prisoners, like professors or company presidents who get fired, should get severance pay. We felt we should think in terms of a severance allowance for these prisoners. We also added the notion that there should be bonuses and incentives on top of the severance pay for actually getting a job. The severance pay says the prisoner is entitled to a certain amount that is paid out to him over a period of three months. And the bonus assumption is that you're entitled to extra money if you manage to get a job within the three-month period.

We made these proposals in our book. But they were not regarded with terribly much favor by the Department of Labor, our sponsors, on the grounds that it departed too much from their assigned bureaucratic concerns. Their concerns were to fold this program into another existing program that they administered, the unemployment insurance system. If you put the proposals as I did, as a severance pay system, then probably the most appropriate place to administer that type of payment was through the prison system which could operate under different rules than the unemployment security system. So what we came up with in the way of viable recommended policy, one that would incorporate the experience of the two sets of experiments, from Baltimore and from Texas and Georgia, was not terribly attractive to the Department of Labor. It didn't fit into their plans and their way of operating. They preferred a recommended policy which would be integrated with their existing system much more easily.

Of course, I wasn't myself terribly convinced that this policy would actually work, whether the payments were called severance pay or not. After all, a disincentive effect arises from the fact that if you need some income and you get it as a gift without working, if working is inherently painful or unpleasant (and the jobs that these released prisoners were likely to get are usually unpleasant and painful) then there's a disincentive to work. We have to know more about the positive incentives for working. Besides, a policy of this sort would immediately raise equity issues. The ordinary law-abiding citizen who finds himself out of work is treated quite differently. He doesn't get the gift and this bonus.

Given all of these possibilities, which I should like to see explored in further experiments, the interest of the Department of Labor dropped very rapidly. Furthermore, just when I had convinced Howard Rosen that there might possibly be something in what I was recommending and he decided to take me to see the Secretary of Labor, Mr. Ray Marshall, about it, the Carter Administration decided that they were going to adopt a general austerity program. Marshall, as a trained economist, understood our microeconomic theory and the analysis resulting from it and he was sympathetic to the whole idea, but it was too late. The administration was too busy for the next nine months to bother with the experiments and the recommended policy. I think the whole episode of the experiments has just disappeared from the institutional memory of the Department of Labor. It's interesting to see the reasons why our policy suggestions were not acted upon.

That was at the federal level. At the state level, things were a little different. One of the legislators in California, knowing about the Baltimore experiments and ours, introduced legislation implementing a plan of the kind we suggested for his state. And it has been in effect since then. He was a very conservative legislator who understood, as he said, "the meaning of money" as an incentive for released prisoners not to commit crime and to look for work. The legislator, a Mr. Behr, managed to get his plan through the California legislature, and the odd thing is that it works in that state. It has been evaluated and the evaluation shows that it has some positive effects on recidivism. The evaluation study was done by my collaborator, Richard Berk. The study required only a small amount of money and was actually funded by the federal Department of Labor. The study was able to take advantage of an unintended natural experiment. The California legislation had stipulated that eligibility for the program be determined by the number of days worked in prison. But the prison system did not administer the program according to this stipulation. They apparently gave out the eligibility almost at random. That meant that the prisoners had not been able to self-select themselves into the eligible class because they didn't know in advance that working in prison was going to make them eligible. In the natural experiment that the evaluation took advantage of, it was possible to hold constant the selection process by which people were or were not eligible for payments. It turned out that the people who did get the payments were less likely to get re-arrested in the year after release by about the same amount as the Baltimore prisoners were. So the policy has about a 5 to 8 percent disincentive effect on recidivism.

For various value and economic austerity reasons, of course, the Reagan Administration has had no interest in this program. And, seemingly for austerity reasons again, other states have not followed California's lead. There might have been more diffusion if the federal Depart-

ment of Labor had continued its interest; but it didn't. The prison
system and the unemployment security system in California liked the
program, even when we informed them of our original negative effects,
because it increased their authority and gave them more work to do.
They had certain programmatic views and they felt this fitted in, even if
it wasn't clear what the effects would be. The prison system liked it because it gave them another sanction on the prisoners. They thought that
they could better control the prisoners by denying them work and
thereby effecting their eligibility for payments on release. Both the
prison and the unemployment security system liked the fact that they
could hire more people to administer the program. All the agencies responsible for dealing with social problems get to have a vested interest
in that problem; it's almost as if they want to see the problem increased. They have some tendency to exaggerate the problem. You
could almost say that a new industry arises around each social problem
and that may have been what was happening in the California case.

There were a number of ways planned and actually used by which
our study was supposed to exert its influence on policy. I have already
mentioned the aborted plan for congressional lobbying and the planned
media publicity effort by the American Bar Association. They had
planned an hour-long television documentary and they had been in
touch with Representative Conyers, the black congressman from Detroit,
who was head of the committee in the House that deals with Department of Labor legislation. He is a prominent member of the Black
Caucus in the House. All that never happened as planned. Another
mode of influence was the publication of our monograph[1] (dedicated to
"Howard Rosen: Devoted, Persistent, and Innovative Civil Servant"). This
was written in a peculiar way, different from most academic mono-
graphs, in order to maximize its policy influence. It is written three
times. The first chapter is written telegraphically, it's what is usually
called "an executive summary," intended for the busy policy-making
person, either a legislator or someone in the executive branch of government. The next four chapters were intended to be an intelligent layman's report, something like what might appear in *Scientific American.*
It's not terribly technical but still technically correct. The last segment of
the book is the completely technical underpinning for the whole study.
This way of writing the book was a deliberate effort to make it available
for policy-makers. Indeed, one of our initial plans was to publish the

[1] Peter H. Rossi, Richard A. Berk, and Kenneth J. Lenihan, *Money, Work, and Crime: Experimental Evidence* (New York: Academic Press, 1980).

first chapter separately in addition to doing the whole monograph. We
wanted to distribute that separate part to members of the Congress and
such people. Howard Rosen was committed to this idea, but nothing
ever came of it, partly because he retired about this time, a little sooner
than he had expected. An invoice to purchase 500 reprints of the first
chapter and 200 copies of the whole book had actually been prepared
in the Department of Labor, but the invoice was canceled after Rosen's
retirement. Also, remember, this was in the later part of the Carter Administration and the early part of the Reagan Administration, in both of
which periods there was a lot of emphasis on austerity. In addition, in
the early part of the Reagan Administration there was a lot of hostility
to social science in general. Our study was exactly the kind of study that
would have been criticized by the Reagan Administration as the kind of
thing that leads to undermining the moral fiber of our society, the kind
of thing that promotes homosexuality, crime, drugs, and other dangers
like herpes and AIDS. I had some contact in the early part of the
Reagan Administration with various agencies and some of the new people were really ranting against social science.

As a result of all these factors and this opposition, we never got to
testify before Congress. We had, of course, briefed Secretary Marshall,
but nothing came of that for the reasons I've mentioned. And, oddly
enough, there aren't any pro-prisoner advocacy groups we could influence. The John Howard Society is devoted to helping prisoners, but
mostly when they're still in prison. It's very weak. They are themselves
ex-prisoners. Although ex-prisoners constitute a fairly large aggregate in
our society, they are not joined together in any solidarity associations.
Nobody really wants it to be known that he is an ex-prisoner. Among
lawyers, the criminal bar has an interest only in individual prisoners,
their clients, not in ex-prisoners as a class.

If our policy recommendations had been accepted, we would probably have had to deal with newspaper and TV publicity. I've done that for
other studies, but I don't like that role. In this study, I would probably
have asked Ken Lenihan to do it. Dealing with the media is a very frus-
trating role for me, very time-consuming, and you have to have more
tolerance for oral communication than I have. I don't even feel it's all
that worthwhile to go down to Washington to testify before a group of
staff people. I'm not terribly good at it and it's not, therefore, a very
effective use of my time. One of my troubles is that I'm always somewhat skeptical about my studies. I'm aware of all the qualifications the
studies need and I believe it's only responsible to make those qualifications public. I feel the same way about all social science work, so I have

difficulty in rallying around to support social science when it's being attacked. Having served for three years on the National Science Foundation peer review panels, I would say that two thirds of the research that's funded isn't worth funding. I don't want to have to say that in public when social science is so unfairly under challenge. Some people are much better as public communicators than I am. For example, Ken Lenihan is good at it. In this study, he speaks from a real conviction about the substantive area and from a sympathy with the prisoners and their really serious problems. I myself don't like the prisoners; they're ghastly. I guess I like them in the abstract, but not individually. And as for social science in general, Kenneth Prewitt, the president of the Social Science Research Council, can speak with a lot more conviction than I can. I just don't have that.

One other way in which our study did have some influence. There were about a dozen or so other people who were doing research and writing in this area and we helped and counseled them. We were also in touch with some of the committees of the National Research Council that deal with crime and also with the people at the National Institute of Justice. There's been a continuing interest in recidivism and its reduction and a cost effective way of reducing it. We still say that the policy we recommended is probably less costly per unit of effect than almost anything else that people have thought of. But this is not in the least convincing to lots of people, including the head of the National Institute of Justice. The current head, Chip Stewart, brought together a whole group of those of us who are doing criminological research and asked us to advise on the kinds of programs the institute should start that would make some significant dent on crime. My collaborator, Dick Berk, and I went to that meeting and advocated doing something about released prisoners because they're a significant source of crime in the United States. But they wanted something more dramatic than what we had to offer, something that would prevent crime before it even began, not the crime that convicted criminals might commit.

These two excursions got me interested in the area and also a certain visibility as a worker in the field. From the elite opinion study we devised a measure of the seriousness of crime. Such a measure was necessary for any policy that was going to recommend community confinement as against regular prison incarceration. But I have to say that all this happened, my doing the research, only because Howard Rosen was in trouble on that one, too, and needed someone who was a general research expert. Here again I was being the "study doctor." Although there is a criminology research community that centers around the

American Society of Criminology and other professional associations, I'm not a part of that community or a member of those associations. I really don't want to be. There's some resentment from the criminology specialists that I have done these studies but am not a member of their community.

These specialists show other kinds of resistance to our study of recidivism. Some of the criminologists don't like the microeconomic analysis I used and have felt that I'm selling out to the economists. They also feel that it doesn't address the "basic" causes of crime but deals only with superficial aspects of it and therefore doesn't really contribute to our understanding of the crime problem. They feel it doesn't get at the central issues, the social conditions or the personal conditions which give rise to criminal behavior. Then there is the methodological opposition of Hans Zeisel, who was on our advisory board and who felt strongly enough that he expressed his views in an article in the *American Journal of Sociology*, to which I replied. When he saw the draft of our report, he said he didn't like the style of my analysis. He wanted two-variable analysis, with bar graphs and cross-tabulations. He didn't like my multivariate analysis. He was also offended because, having been one of my patrons in the early days when I was at the University of Chicago, he didn't like to have his advice rejected. His article started out as a memo to me but finally became a published polemic. But his style of analysis was no longer my style. His style was all right for the 1950s but not for the present, given all the sophisticated advances in methodology that have been made.

I think he also has a strong substantive objection to our work. He has a very deep conviction that crime is not something that you can do anything about other than incarcerate criminals. His ideological position is very conservative as opposed to my more liberal one. His article says that if there's anything we've learned in the last thirty years in criminology it's that even a generous payment to released prisoners won't work. As for other criminologists and sociologists of law besides Zeisel, their resistance comes from their conviction that we're not dealing with the causes of crime. They're right. We're recommending administrative fixes that will alleviate some of the crime. They're more concerned with preventive medicine, at least some of them are. All I'm doing comes from a different paradigm. It says, we don't touch the crime, we just alter the situation slightly so that it becomes easier for the person to give up crime. What I'm doing is much more policy-oriented and much less a derivative of general social science and its understanding of the general sources of social behavior.

Besides the criminologists, there were some people who expressed objections based on value and equity issues. They didn't want special treatment for ex-prisoners; they didn't want people "rewarded" for having gone to jail. People think that the unemployment security system is an entitlement system, they approve of that, and they don't want released prisoners to be entitled in the same way as the regularly unemployed. For example, the *National Enquirer* found out about our study and its recommendations and wrote a story, with big headlines, called "Cash for Crooks." They said that a new program of the Department of Labor would be a give-away to crooks when they get out of prison.

When someone on Senator Proxmire's staff saw this story, he felt we would be good candidates for their "Golden Fleece Award," which is Senator Proxmire's way of publicizing what he, or his staff, thinks are trivial or foolish social science studies. Someone on his staff went to the Department of Labor for the details of both its support and our study and were about to give this Golden Fleece Award to the Department of Labor and to me and my colleagues. We felt it would be nice to have the award, but since our study was still out in the field in Georgia and Texas and we were afraid that those states might become nervous and end the study, we decided to try to do something about it. I spent about three days in Washington, along with Ken Lenihan, trying to convince Proxmire's staff that the study and the program had some really potential good to it. We argued that the cost savings that were given by the results of the LIFE experiment in Baltimore were large and important. Believe it or not, we finally talked them out of their intention to give us the award. But that whole experience showed some of the value resistance to the program and to our study.

What have I learned from this study and from all the other studies I've done that have had policy relevance? I've certainly learned that what I originally thought about the connection between social science and the policy-maker isn't so at all. The initial connection which I thought would exist, if we ever got into a situation in which the social sciences were trusted, was one in which the social scientist sat at the side of the policy-maker and handed him a piece of paper which told him what to say and do. That is to say, I thought the social scientist would be a technical expert who illuminates the legislation and the administrative regulations which the policy-maker promulgates. Nothing like that is the case. The initial reaction to realizing this is one of terrible disappointment. There was a period of time, during the 1960s, when the social scientists were welcomed in Washington and regarded highly, but my notion of sitting at the elbow of and becoming the adviser to the policy-maker did not materialize. I came to realize my disappointment was naive. As I thought about it later, I realized I didn't want it that way, I didn't want policy issues to be settled by policy experts. They ought to be settled by the political process, that is to say, by the interplay of interests illuminated by the information that experts can bring to both sides of a political process, of a political struggle. So I see a much more modest role for the social scientists now than I did originally; it is a role in which the objective truth seems to be more and more dimly defined. There is no set of empirical findings which are not subject to some degree of challenge from the point of view of the theoretical definitions from which their measurements flow. I didn't use to see that. I thought that all social scientists, sitting around a table, could come to the same definition of a given phenomenon. Now I see that the definition is somewhat constrained by the world out there but that there's a lot of give and take and play in those definitions. Value considerations play a part and different theoretical orientations play a strong role. So that social science is not just one piece of fabric but lots of different views. I'm no longer very sanguine about how important a role social science can play. Of course, one can think that providing different social science perspectives is important. I'm beginning to believe that that is the case. What we do by entering the advocacy arena is to sharpen and clarify the issues. That doesn't mean we determine the outcome. What we do is shift the universe of discourse surrounding a particular issue. It's a much more modest role and one which I now find, after much soul searching and squelching of ambitions, to be not bad.

I should say that I made a statement of this kind to my students and found they got very upset. Those who believe in the old science model felt that there must be some objective truth that everybody with the same abilities and intelligence could arrive at. Others were upset because my view seemed to lead to a kind of relativism of knowledge, a sociology of knowledge box of the Mannheim variety, where everything is relative and so we can abandon ethics and science and method, values and all. I don't think either of those two positions is correct. My position is one that is hard for the typical American graduate student to accept.

It follows from my position that knowledge is not a necessary and very powerful tool in social and political processes. And my viewpoint makes it difficult to be effective politically; you have to be a believer. It's hard to engage in heavy participation in the political process on that basis. I've come to think that values are more important than knowledge. I want someone to represent me who has my values, not my knowledge.

As for the processes of social change in society, I started out here, too, rather simply, thinking that they were easy to understand and easy to bring about. Now society sometimes looks to me more like a system which lurches blindly along some path which is dimly illuminated. I don't know whether that means that we're unable to understand the complicated system or whether the system does not have sufficient permanence and solidity to it. So much seems random or arbitrary capricious movement, some of it driven by outside forces, some by processes where we can't see connections. I've observed the political scene in Washington for a twenty-year period, 1960 to 1980. Lots happened. But I can't make rhyme or reason out of it. I can't understand the enormous cultural revolution that we've had. Sometimes I think I can understand the sixteenth to eighteenth centuries better than 1960 to 1980. But that may be illusionary. Maybe if I knew as much about the sixteenth to eighteenth centuries as I know about 1960 to 1980, I would be equally confused. Still, I feel you can do something about social change, but not very much and you'll never know if you'll succeed or fail. The rules for achieving social change are not easily grasped. We don't know the leverage points.

Chapter Eight

Alan F. Westin

The Protection of Privacy
in the Public and Private Sectors

*Alan F. Westin, professor of public law and government at Co-
lumbia University, may have had more influence on law, practice,
and public policy with regard to the issue of privacy than any
other single person in the United States during the last thirty years.
His career-long involvement in research, writing, and activism in
this field has extended to both the governmental and private sectors. He has advised congressmen and corporate leaders alike,
and his efforts in educating the general public in the privacy aspects of the contemporary technological and social era have also
been extensive.*

Interview: July 1984

My interest in political science began very early. As an undergraduate at
the University of Florida, I came under the influence of two excellent
political scientists, William G. Carlton and Manning Dauer. Their approach to American politics was institutionalist and theoretical. I was
only 18 when I graduated from college, and went directly to the Harvard Law School. There I decided very early that I wanted to be a
scholar in law and politics rather than a practicing attorney, but that was
not quite to be what happened. I became both a scholar and a policy

advocate. At Harvard my bent ran toward constitutional law and civil liberties. I was exceptionally fortunate in coming under the tutelage of Paul Freund, the distinguished constitutional scholar, and Mark DeWolfe Howe, the noted scholar in American legal history. Arthur Sutherland was a warm and helping professor with whom I did the first piece of work that set me on the privacy path. I chose to write a paper on wiretapping; Sutherland found it excellent and encouraged me to publish it, and that launched my privacy career.

After law school, I went on to take a Ph.D. in the Harvard Government Department, where again I was fortunate in my mentors. Robert McClosky's combined interest in constitutional law and political theory was valuable in forming my ideas and perspectives. Louis Hartz was then laying out, in graduate seminars, his seminal views on the liberal tradition in America. I was also glad to discover Charles Cherington, who also had the L.L.B.-Ph.D. combination and had chosen full-time university teaching. His advice was "talk law to the political scientists and political science to the lawyers, and you'll prosper with both disciplines."

Both my law and my political science training, on balance, pushed me toward emphasizing the empirical more than the theoretical aspects of scholarship. I have learned from reading Justice Holmes' *The Common Law* that the growth of law is best understood by deep historical analysis of how legal rules are enunciated out of the interplay of new policy problems and the values of various law-speakers such as judges and legislators. I also felt that a greater concentration on interest group use of litigation and legal processes was essential to an understanding of how legal and political ideas get developed, advocated, and promoted in the American government system.

As a result of these dispositions, I have tended to choose social problems for study that were interesting to me as emerging social problems rather than choosing examples to explore or illuminate some theoretical scheme. And I have been eclectic in the theories I have applied to the problems I've selected to explore. For example, I was quite far along in my interest in the problem of new threats of technology to privacy before I had anything like a coherent theory of its place in the social order or in the political and legal systems. I began by assembling heavily empirical descriptions of the privacy environment—what people and groups were doing with new technology and how this was affecting traditional privacy interests. I didn't start off by formulating a set of theoretical statements. However, before I could write the book about privacy that I found myself called to write, as director in 1963–67 of a project sponsored by the Association of the Bar of the City of New York (funded by the Rockefeller Foundation), I had to search through history, political science, sociology, law, anthropology, psychology, psychiatry, and so on for useful theoretical frameworks to illuminate my problem. I guess I'm an applied social scientist looking for clarity and supports through theory, rather than a theoretician who goes to find proof of his theory.

My primary interest in social problems in general and in civil liberties in particular had its origin in my very early political orientation. I started off as a young man with a left of center political orientation. I first saw myself as Wallace Progressive, as a political activist. Both at the University of Florida and at the Harvard Law School, I was quite active in social change organizations that were challenging the dominant political and economic ideas of that time. So it's not surprising that the problems I have chosen to work on are matters where I see American values related to the rights and interests of minorities, political dissenters, and cultural nonconformists needing to be illuminated by research, and thereby strengthening policy actions designed to help such groups. For example, when I was an undergraduate, Florida was an absolutely segregated state; I was a participant in integration and civil rights activities. I picketed and demonstrated against the southern governors when they met on our campus in 1947 and 1948. I felt then and still feel a passionate commitment to freedom of speech, freedom of the press, freedom of association, individual rights to privacy, and similar basic liberties of a democratic society.

As early as when I was in law school, I realized I had to make a choice of how to express my commitment. I had a close personal friend who shared many of my ideas and with whom I discussed the common choice that confronted us. He decided to leave the Harvard Law School and go to work in a factory as an undercover agent for the Communist party. He chose the radical activist role. I drew back from that and, for what I am sure is a combination of rational and personality-based reasons, decided that I would make my contribution through scholarship, and through social advocacy based on speech and writing, rather than direct action.

One of the hallmarks of my work on civil liberties and other social problems these last thirty years has been following an instinctive feeling about major changes beginning in society. I have found it challenging to try to identify them, to give them contours, and to specify clearly the value and policy choices that our society is going to have to make as these changes take place. Such an early identification of emerging prob-

lems has been my experience about six or eight times since the early
1950s. For example, when I was in graduate school, I wrote several papers on diplomatic relations with the Vatican. That was a topic that interested me because it involved a combination of legal problems (the
separation of church and state) and also political science issues of inter-
religious–group conflict, public administration, and U.S. foreign policy
goals and processes. When I first wrote about this problem, in 1952, the
United States was entering a period of drastic change in the status of
American Catholics and in the thinking of the Vatican. It was the beginning of the great "window opening" in the Papacy. Another example
was research and writing that I did on the John Birch Society and the
radical right in 1960–62. Still a third example is the trend toward new
individual rights of nonunion employees in the corporation which I
started working on in the mid-1950s, returned to as a major research
activity in the late 1970s, and am now once again deeply engaged in.

My work has not been influenced by an interest in technical methodological concerns. But I have thought of myself as having a definite
and repeated methodology for all the technology-society subjects I've
worked on, such as the privacy, due process, and freedom of information issues affected by computers and information technology. I like to
start by laying a historical baseline, a description of what the institutions
and values and processes were before the new technology came along.
I describe how much uniformity and diversity there was in these
baseline patterns and who was advantaged or disadvantaged by the
power and interests resulting from these patterns. When I did my first
book on privacy, published in 1967, I felt I had to trace the development of privacy as a concept from primitive to modern times in order
to see what was distinctive and new about the nineteenth- and early
twentieth-century notions of privacy and how these were going to be
affected by new technological options.

I'm doing the same thing for my present work on office systems technology and how this will affect work, workers, and work organizations.
What I try to construct is a way of identifying and measuring how any
new technology will develop from the baseline, how it will either
change or consolidate the existing power and value structure. I don't
think of methodology so much in the sense of choosing to use either
quantitative or qualitative data or whether interview or documentary
analysis are inherently "better." And in the large-scale projects I've developed and directed, I've always used a mixture of survey techniques
to map broad trends, in-depth interviewing and case studies to get to
operating realities and analysis of interests, values, and social balances
to add the normative dimensions.

As I've already indicated, the value issues in my research have always been very important to me. An image or model of society and its values that Paul Freund used in one of his lectures at Harvard Law School has stuck with me as a guide. He said you can think of society, social values, and social change in terms of a Newtonian model of action, reaction, and dynamic equilibrium. There are always plenty of conservative forces insisting that there be no social change, and why efforts at a larger realization of equality or liberty or justice will present lots of problems. So, there needs to be sharp advocates on the other side, asserting these values, advocating them, and documenting why the status quo is no longer acceptable. As advocates of change, these people don't always present the wisest or best positions that might ultimately be adopted. But somebody's got to be out there pressing for positions that are more egalitarian, or more civil libertarian, so that a compromise, reformist position can be achieved.

With this model in mind, and given my commitment to civil liberties, I joined activist groups like the American Civil Liberties Union, the American Jewish Congress, and a variety of others to help push for more egalitarian or more libertarian social policies. Somebody had to be a zealous advocate of these values. After a while, though, I found myself wanting to be not so much the advocate as trying to help define and structure the choices society was making about the desirable balance or equilibrium of values. I wanted to find out what needed to be known about egalitarian and libertarian values and social processes affecting them. I felt the best way to use my knowledge was to speak directly, if I could, to the chief decision-makers in the society, to show them how to accommodate the status quo forces and the social change forces. Through the kind of research problems I chose, through the organizational positions I took, through publications, public advocacy, and expert testimony, I've tried to sensitize decision-makers to the fact that they often weren't considering the right problems. I also tried to present them with practical ways to address the real concerns of people for privacy, due process, equality, free expression, and so forth. I believe my basic values and goals have remained the same, but I've changed my tactics in seeking to realize them. I think it's interesting that my birth sign is Libra, the classic scale holder, signifying balance: on the one hand this, on the other, that. I feel myself to be a Libra, committed to definite values but a weigher of alternative positions and tactics.

In addition to being concerned about general values, I've always tried to formulate specific policy goals and identify practical ways of achieving them. For example, in the very first of my published papers, "The Wiretapping Problem: An Analysis, and a Legislative Proposal," published in the *Columbia Law Review* in 1952, I concluded the paper with a statutory proposal. The paper was a historical, empirical account of the widespread use of wiretapping in American society and a statement of how dangerous it was that we didn't have any legal controls on it. I explained, as a social analyst, the reasons why our legal system was so indecisive about wiretapping, and our ambivalence as to permit it through administrative discretion, to ban it altogether or to set a middle course, allowing some wiretapping under independent, judicial safeguards. Because of the legal stalemate caused by a failure to resolve these different positions, I pointed out, there was a wholesale violation of privacy and government lawlessness that was very dangerous to a democratic society. In that article, as in all I've written since, I've felt it was my obligation not simply to reveal and describe the problem but to come up with a way of resolving it. So I drafted a model statute that faced the choices that had to be made about how to use wiretapping. It prescribed tightly controlled circumstances for limited wiretapping and indicated ways of anticipating and coping with the excesses and problems that might occur. My suggested statute contained specific safeguards and a variety of institutional and publicity measures for the desired middle course.

Within a couple of years, the proposal that I made in that article became legislation in two states, Oregon and Maryland. Subsequently, I had the fascinating experience of having a judge in Oregon write to me and say that since he was deciding a case based on the statute that was based on my article, he wanted to know what I had intended as "the framer" of the statute. I replied that he would have to decide what the *Oregon Legislature* had intended, but did tell him how I would decide the case he was considering if it had come before me as a judge.

I can't think of many things that I write which don't end up with very concrete recommendations to people who hold power, as well as to those advocates who are trying to change the distribution of power. New organizational policies, new laws, new executive actions, new uses of money, new research agendas—these have always seemed to me the moral requirement of the kind of policy research and writing that I do. That was certainly the case in the research on possible abuses of computers and data banks that I'll describe later.

I don't think I've changed my purpose over the years, but my approach has gotten more and more specific, and I've been more concerned increasingly with implementations analyses.

Because I have been an activist as well as a scholar in the field of civil liberties, I have been asked how my activism affected my research.

I remember that when I was starting out as a young political scientist I made a very conscious judgment that it was important for me to be *inside* organizations that were the leading edge of change in the civil liberties field. They were a gold mine of invaluable empirical information about the problems of their—and my—concern. Going to their meetings, reading their materials, listening to their accounts of negotiations with government and corporations and unions on matters of discrimination or abuse of power all gave me a pipeline into reality that was otherwise unavailable. That was especially true back in the 1950s when you did not get the superb, in-depth coverage of civil liberties and civil rights issues that you get today in the mass media and a wide array of specialized publications. Back in the forties and fifties, one had to scrounge for information about violations of liberties. Going into the activist organizations put me directly in touch with what was going on.

Although the issues have changed, I still feel that, as a scholar, I have to be in the change-oriented organizations that are relevant to the issues I want to explore. So I do consulting work, I go to the leading-edge national and international conferences on these topics, to keep up with new ideas. So often, what is published is already out of date by the time it appears. To be at the edge of new data and new ideas, you have to be in the active organizations themselves. They are the ones that are collecting the best information and formulating new definitions of the problems I'm interested in. I have spent a lot of time in this way that otherwise I couldn't justify to myself. There are so damned many meetings, and it's not pleasant seeing people beating one another's brains out over ideological or organizational matters. It's often an enormous waste of time, and not congenial to my personality. I did it, and still do it selectively because I get so much information not otherwise available.

In all of this, let me note, I was not what sociologists call a participant observer. On a scale with participant at one end and observer at the other, I would locate my role about at the middle. I did not see myself in these organizations *primarily* to influence or make policy, though I sometimes did that on particular issues that I especially cared about. I was very much seeing the organizations as enormously valuable resources for information about what was going on and for knowledge about the social role and dynamics of those organizations. Many times I did feel myself just watching the people in the organizations rather than being ready to commit myself totally to what they were debating and deciding.

The resources for my research and other activities have come from a very wide variety of sources. As to government sources, I've received only limited support from local or state governments. The kinds of problems I've worked on and the social policies I've been interested in are not the traditional ones for those levels of government to support. However, when I was directing a center on civic education jointly sponsored by Columbia University and Teachers College, a center concerned with what should be the content and process of American elementary and secondary education, we did get resources of cooperation, staff, and even a little money from the local school districts and from some state and local education agencies. But mostly, on the government side, it has been federal agency funds that have supported my work. For example, in connection with my Center for Research and Education in American Liberties, between 1965 and 1971 we got about $2 million from the National Defense Education Act program to run training programs for teachers, do basic research on how American liberties were changing, help those who run the educational system to rethink both the content of education and what students' rights should be, and, finally, to consider how schools operate and how that might be changed. I've also had funding support from the Department of Education, the National Endowment for the Humanities, the National Science Foundation, the U.S. Office of Technology Assessment, and the Department of Justice. Thus, some of this federal support has been from agencies with specific programmatic interests that coincided with mine; others have been grants for more basic research as from the National Science Foundation.

Early on, I accepted the way in which our society offers scholars support from foundations. I have been fortunate enough to have received grants from a couple of dozen of the major foundations for a wide variety of research projects, ranging from working on a judicial biography to researching civil rights law issues. I've received grants from such foundations as the Carnegie Corporation, the Fund for the Republic, the Walter E. Meyer Institute of Law, the New World Foundation, the Rockefeller Foundation, the Russell Sage Foundation. Some of the foundations have supported different projects over a long period of time. For example, the Russell Sage Foundation was early interested in my work at the intersection of law and social science. They supported the research for the *Data Banks in a Free Society* study. And currently, they are supporting my work on due process mechanisms in nonunion employment and in the corporate world. There have been a wide range of small, medium, and large foundations that have supported everything from small, well-focused, short-term kinds of work to projects that took two, three, or five years to complete.

Many of the nonprofit voluntary organizations that I belonged to, and others as well, have opened doors for me in my research or have made their archives available. For example, when I wrote a book, with a colleague, called *The Trial of Martin Luther King,* which was an account of one constitutional law case, *Walker* v. *Birmingham,* I got all the cooperation I needed from civil rights organizations. They got me access to people and let me see their papers. Professional associations, civic and political groups, and historical societies have been helpful in my research. There have also been a variety of trade and occupational associations, who assisted when I have worked in their fields: The American Federation of Information Processing Societies, the Association for Computing Machinery, and the Computer Business Equipment Manufacturers Association. The insurance industry has been willing to show me their studies of how they use computers to process people's claims and benefits. Often these are not published studies; they have been done by inside staff who will sit down to talk, and who will also refer me to other people inside the industry. Organizations of all kinds, from radical and activist to the most establishment types, have been vital resources for my work. To obtain such access, you have to be credible, to be seen as someone who is going to put their information to a use which is not biased or distorted, but fairly reflects their experiences and viewpoints. If you have that reputation, all sorts of windows and doors are opened.

I've also had considerable help from individual business firms. One of the facts I learned very early was that there are certain kinds of companies in the United States which, taking a fairly broad sense of their corporate interests and image, will sponsor a considerable amount of research that is publicly oriented, not as proprietary work or as consultation, but to be available to the general public. And several dozen of these firms have given me detailed access to their own operations when my research overlapped with their problems and concerns. For example, for my *Data Banks in a Free Society,* the findings of which I'll describe later, I had access to IBM, Bank of America, Mutual of Omaha, Control Data Corporation, Citibank, Aetna Life and Casualty, and so forth. I wanted to see how the use of computer technology in the late 1960s and early 1970s was affecting privacy and due process rights. In other research work, I have been interested in corporate policies toward blacks, or women, or hiring in general, or in corporate internal complaint systems for their employees, and I've been able to get deeply into the firms that I wanted to study, sometimes by guaranteeing anonymity for them but often in producing scholarly products that allowed organizational identities to be disclosed. I believe strongly that such identification needs to be sought as often as possible so that other scholars and the media can test and judge the conclusions of my research.

While I was doing the *Data Banks* study, I had no financial relationship with these firms. But afterwards, when companies had organizational interest in some study I was doing, I obtained financial support for my projects. For example, Exxon sponsored one of my studies—how to use large-scale computer systems to bring together exposure data and medical data on employees working with dangerous chemicals, coordinated with epidemiological research on the effects of toxic substances. These expensive, two-to-three-million-dollar computer systems are indispensable for the systematic collection, analysis, modeling, and simulation procedures necessary for such a study. However, our tort law provides large disincentives for companies to do such studies, because the studies might be used against them in suits alleging that an employer "had knowledge" of harmful conditions and did not prevent harm. There is a dilemma here. On the one hand, innovative use of the new information technology can make it possible for organizations to be more responsible and more anticipative of dangers to their employees and others; on the other hand, our law and our rewards system for lawyers makes that difficult, given the present climate of high litigation. Some of my research has been sponsored by firms wanting help in resolving dilemmas of this kind. Presumably, these companies realize that I already know a lot about a problem, that I can do systematic research on several companies, and that I can suggest responsible solutions that could satisfy all the participants on the issue: workers, unions, occupational health and safety officers, etc. Frequently, I have organized meetings at which companies interested in a given problem can come together and share their experiences, sometimes with only corporations present and sometimes with all the adversary interests participating. Having heard from all the interested groups, my colleagues and I come up with a report that points to a balance among the various duties, rights, regulations, and incentives that are present. I have found that a small but important core of individual business firms, especially through the professionals responsible for these problems in the firms, are willing to sponsor quite venturesome research and activity, if they have the confidence that what's going to come out of it is a contribution to public understanding of their problems.

One kind of support and resource that has been especially important for my research has been the creation of advisory panels of organizational representatives to help assure the proper coverage and treatment of policy-oriented social research. For one thing, funding organizations are more receptive if they see people from a variety of interests and ideologies coming together to work on a problem. I have used such advisory boards to check, test, and improve the ideas that we started with, or to probe the adequacy of the information we acquired through research. This "diversity" approach has been especially useful in my field of civil liberties, such as privacy and due process, where there are indeed a variety of relevant interests and values. In the 1950s and the early 1960s, such advisory committees helped my projects to get access to important bodies of government and private-sector information that would otherwise have been unavailable.

The *Data Banks* study is a good example of the value of these cooperative organizations for my work. I knew I had to get deep into such places as the FBI and the Social Security Administration in government, and into private organizations such as Bank of America or the Kaiser Permanente Health System. Having the sponsorship of the National Academy of Sciences (and a grant from the Russell Sage Foundation) helped secure access into these and other government organizations that didn't have to let me in by law, or were powerful enough private organizations to deny just about anybody access. And, even when the federal Freedom of Information Act, passed in 1966 and expanded in 1974, allows scholars to get access to vital documents, that still doesn't ensure access to the interviews with officials that much of my research called for.

In the 1950s and early 1960s, I had been pretty much operating as an individual scholar. Sometimes I was linked with an organization like the Association of the Bar of the City of New York, which had a Select Committee on Science and Privacy, and which brought me in to direct the study which produced my book *Privacy and Freedom* in 1967. After that appeared, I was invited by a very gifted scholar and policy-consultant, Professor Anthony Oettinger of Harvard, to serve on a committee he chaired, the Computer Science and Engineering Board of the National Academy of Sciences. That board was a great learning experience for me, because it had on it first-class people from business groups like IBM and Digital Equipment Corporation and outstanding scholars in the fields of physics and computing. There were also members from key professional associations and government agencies. The committee identified computer data banks as one problem it wanted to work on, and they invited my membership on the board as a social scientist working on the social impact of computers and data banks. Otherwise immovable doors were unlocked for the project I directed for the board on computers and privacy because I carried the imprimatur of the National Academy. And it was invaluable to have, by a collegial process, the review and clearance assistance of the committee. It was quite a disciplining experience. It made me aware of the need to be explicit in the statements of what my staff and I had done and how we did it, why we drew certain conclusions, and why those were justified. Scholars should always try to provide such explicitness, of course, but the NAS process ensures that this is done in a very explicit way. There's a price to be paid for this collegial review process, to be sure; it can force out some of your more venturesome ideas and conclusions. You learn how to develop consensual statements and carefully drawn conclusions for the review process. I found I liked doing some projects this way, but I didn't want to lead my whole research life in this fashion. Sometimes I don't want the committee process, just myself and support staff that I direct, and where I can see that the work goes where I want it to and I can write it up as I please. But for many problems, the format I worked in at the National Academy is both acceptable and probably essential for exploring a particular kind of issue at a particular moment of social concern over what to do about it.

Either as an individual scholar or working with a cooperative group, getting access to otherwise closed sectors requires that certain conditions be met. I suppose there are three keys that I have tried to put in the locks. First, you have to have a reputation for both good scholarship and rational, fully articulated discourse. Then, if someone reads what you have written, they may agree or disagree with you but they have to say that it's well researched, it fairly outlines the problems and weighs the solutions, and is therefore a valuable contribution to policy analysis. I have tried to establish this kind of reputation, so that people will feel that I am likely to understand their point of view, and render it with reasonable faithfulness in anything that is published.

My second key is the protection of confidentiality. If you're doing research on sensitive current events, things that affect people's lives and statuses, you often must make a bargain, an exchange of confidentiality for information. On this basis, I can convince organizations that I need to see all the people who are important to my problem, that I need to see the relevant documentation, and that I need to get my hands on what is really happening. I promise to send them my factual account of what I believe I've found, to let them say whether they think it is complete and accurate, and I will make changes if I agree with them that something has not properly captured events, actions, or professed motives. I don't send my conclusions or judgments for such review. I always separate my descriptive account of organizational actions from the concluding and recommendatory sections at the end. I have no trouble with sending the descriptive part since I know I can be faulty in observation, or in what I draw from interviews, especially since I don't ever tape record the interviews I do. (Many top executives in business and government won't talk to you with a tape recorder going.) Only in a very few cases have organizations said they felt that I had fundamentally misunderstood them and I have never had such an instance that wasn't worked out in further clarifications. Almost always, organizational responses to my drafts have helped my accounts, by pointing out additional facts or giving additional documentation. If you get something three-quarters factually right, organizations have an interest in seeing that you get it all right. So I always work out a carefully designed agreement to let people see what I've written and to guarantee confidentiality where that is needed. However, as I said earlier, I always try to get *representative cases* out in *identified* form, to assure independent verification of any work. In the NAS study we did 55 detailed confidential studies of organizations using computers and then we convinced 14 of those, representative of each sector of record-keeping about people, to let us publish fully identified accounts of their operations. These included both government and private-sector organizations.

The third element in my process has been that most people want to have someone explain why they are doing what they are doing. The world of journalism is often a distorted world, distorted in what it writes about and in how it quotes people. Those who hold significant power in our society, whether in government, the private sector, or even in social-change organizations, can often give you a hundred examples of where journalists have gotten it wrong, haven't understood what they do or say. Some of this complaint is probably self-serving, but when I show people that I can faithfully capture why they are doing things, and since most people believe in what they are doing, they will give me cooperation and access.

Before describing the main findings of my *Data Banks in a Free Society* study, done with the sponsorship and guidance of the National Academy, I need to provide a little background. This is important because the research we did in that study made me change some views I had held earlier on the effects of the new computer technology on privacy. I had started off in the 1950s and early 1960s being interested in the general problem of how technology was affecting a variety of individual rights, especially privacy. When I wrote my first major book, *Privacy and Freedom,* published in 1967, my focus was on new tech-

nologies of physical surveillance, such as wiretapping and electronic
eavesdropping; new technologies of psychological surveillance, such as
personality testing for employment and licensing; and the technologies
of data surveillance, which were then the second and third generation
computer technologies. The motif of the privacy book was that these
new technologies had created new ways in which those who wanted to
invade privacy could do so, and *were* doing so. It seemed to me that
our whole structure of law, which assumed that people could speak and
act privately with reasonable assurance of not being overheard or over-
seen or recorded, was in danger. Walls and distance and darkness no
longer protected privacy. I was fearful of the effects of lie detectors, in-
hibition-releasing substances, and various techniques of emotional stress
measurement that were being used to dissolve established forms of privacy. What I said in the book was that because of the power of these
new technologies, we needed new institutional rules, new definitions of
privacy, and new protective law. My definite but implicit assumption
was that since the new technologies *could* do certain things, therefore
they *would* do them and, indeed, had *already* done these things.

But then I moved on to the data banks study, between 1969 and 1972,
and decided to find out what was actually going on in the specific area
of new technology that was clearly going to be the most pervasive and
powerful, computers and communication systems. I was determined to
visit the organizations that were actually using computers to see what
was really happening, how they were being used, and what demonstra-
ble effects they were having on privacy and due process interests of the
people these organizations were affecting. I realized I hadn't known
much about computers, they were just big black boxes to me, and I had
been relying on what others said their effects were. In my first privacy
study, in the mid-sixties, some of my expert informants had said the
harmful effects were already here, others said such effects were still a
decade away, and others said there was no problem at all and wouldn't
be one. In the privacy book, I had given much greater credibility to
those computer specialists who said the harm was here, now, and to the
journalists and social scientists who had accepted and embellished on
that assumption about computer systems and their uses. I was just dealing with reported phenomena; I hadn't myself gone to see what was
going on.

In the data banks and privacy study, therefore, we selected 55 organizations of various kinds that were reported to us by knowledgeable
people as the ones using the most advanced computer technologies. We
made on-site visits and did case studies of each of these 55 organiza-

tions. We did federal, state, and local government agencies, business corporations, and nonprofit organizations. This research was a revelation to me. It strikingly changed my view of the effects of computers on privacy at that period in time. What I had said in the privacy book, and what I was widely quoted as having said, was that when an organization adopts computer technology, it *automatically* does three things that are harmful, both potentially and actually, to civil liberties, privacy, and due process. First, the organization collects more information about its employees and clients than it did in the manual era. Second, it exchanges and trades this information much more widely with other organizations that have computers than it did before. And, third, once an organization computerizes its data, individuals no longer know where the data are or have access to them to challenge their completeness or accuracy.

As a result of our research in the data banks study, having looked closely at our 55 organizations, I could say that each of these three assumptions was wrong as a statement of present reality. They were not wrong in terms of what computer technology could potentially do but were wrong in terms of what real-world organizations were actually doing then. We discovered that the organizations had a whole series of constraints that kept them from realizing this potential. I had not given proper weight to the fact that these were social organizations enmeshed in a web of legal constraints, organizational jealousies and rivalries, internal competition for power. They were also subject to limits of the market, and to the ability of people not to buy the products of commercial organizations or to cooperate with government organizations if they felt their personal data were being abused. Even when government organizations have a right to demand certain information, they can't prosecute everyone if people choose not to give it. Our research showed us that, at least as of 1971–72, it was still so costly to automate and store data, and the software to manipulate data was still so rudimentary, that most organizations were computerizing only the most frequently used, the most objective, and the most conventionally acceptable information about their clients, customers, subjects, or employees. It was just not true that all kinds of narrative data or soft data were being increasingly automated. Paradoxically, our study found that it was not the top decision-makers in organizations who were lusting after these kinds of data but rather the researchers. It was the researchers in all these organizations who were anxious to know more about their members or customers. Usually they had in mind only pure research, but their desires were often taken to be those of the top administrators of the organizations; and critics were properly worried about whether sensitive data origi-

nally collected for program evaluation would later be used for administrative or regulatory purposes.

We also found that the organizations we studied had always ex-
changed information with those who were like-minded or within an industry or within a conventional network. The computer made it easier
and faster to do this but it wasn't yet creating any new networks. The
local and state police and the FBI had been exchanging fingerprint and
intelligence information since the 1920s; now they were doing so with
computer technology, but they weren't giving that information to Columbia University or the American Civil Liberties Union just because
these places also had computers. The computers by themselves don't
change the patterns of trust, accommodation, and networking. These
patterns are dependent upon lines of social convention, competitive-
ness, and all the other established forces in society. The fact that information can move faster doesn't mean that it then moves in unconven-
tional and apolitical ways.

We also found that what was important about people's access to the
files of data kept about them was not whether it was on tissue paper or
three-by-five cards or computers but whether people were told that a
record was being collected and stored, how it was being used, and how
they could get access to it. In fact, we found that if law or social values
gave individuals the right of access to data, that right could often be
exercised and enforced more easily with a central computer than with
messy manual record systems, often highly decentralized.

As a result of these findings, we concluded our study by saying that
while the three processes we had thought were taking place had not yet
happened in the actual world, these actions both could and probably
would happen unless our society made certain legal and value choices
to forestall these possibilities from actually occurring. If a new set of
legal and institutional norms were not set in place, we said, then computer technology would get cheaper, software would become more
efficient, and organizations would have the incentives to do what we
had found they were not doing yet. We felt there was a moment in time
in the early 1970s in which we could control those computer-technol-
ogy potentials we didn't want to see realized. And we recommended
specific intervention of various kinds to accomplish the goal of preserving fundamental privacy and due process rights in a free society.

Our findings, then, were unexpected and made me change my views
and my recommendations for policy. One other fact about organizations
came to me out of this research in quite a new and forceful way. This

was that the powerful organizations we had studied were also potentially quite vulnerable. I saw that, in our kind of society, if we ever got a revolt of the data-subject masses, not one of our institutions could function effectively. Our society rests on the willingness of millions of us to give our information to banks and credit bureaus and government agents such as tax and law enforcement officials. Of course, the powerful managers of these organizations are not sitting in their offices trembling about the imminent occurrence of such a revolt, a Wat Tyler uprising of the Yuppies, but still they have a tangible incentive to restrain their power and to act in ways that be seen to be just, and that respect privacy and other due process.

This study also had a basic effect on the ways in which I thought about my general problem, the relation between new technologies and civil rights. In *Privacy and Freedom,* I assumed a strong technological determinism. The data banks research made me move to a much more cautious and theoretically different approach. I now came to think of society as a tightly meshed cloth of steel threads made up of law and custom and values and institutions. I thought of technology as a projectile launched against the mesh; it never rips right through, but makes a complex passage in which the web reshapes the projectile and is itself rearranged by the projectile going through it. I think of this as a "soft determinist" approach, since I assume that the technological projectiles are rarely if ever wholly repulsed.

As a result of the data banks research and other research that I've done both on the national scene and in particular organizational situations, I think I can say that my work has had a variety of social effects. I've recommended laws and those laws have been passed; I've recommended creating commissions and those commissions have been created; I've formulated codes for organizations to promulgate voluntarily—organizations such as hospitals, universities, corporations—and those codes have been adopted. So far as laws are concerned, for example, as the consultant to the Senate Government Operations Committee, I assisted Senator Ervin in the development of the bill that was ultimately enacted as the Federal Privacy Act of 1974. As for commissions, I've suggested or served on or been consulted by such commissions as the American Jewish Committee's Commission on Law, Social Action, and Urban Affairs, the National Commission for the Review of Federal and State Laws Relating to Wiretapping and Electronic Surveillance, and the New Jersey State Commission on Individual Liberty and Personal Privacy. Finally, by way of example, as to formulating codes for private organizations, I've been a consultant on codes on employee privacy policy for such companies as IBM, Allied Chemical, Sentry Insurance, Nabisco, and Security Pacific National Bank.

A lot of my effort has gone to help raise public consciousness about the civil liberties issues I'm interested in. I've done this in several ways. First, I've spent a lot of time publicizing these issues in the media. In print media, for example, I've written articles and reviews for the *New York Times* (Magazine, Book Review, and Business sections), the *New Leader, Commentary, American Heritage,* the *New Republic,* the *Nation,* the *Saturday Review, Playboy, Fortune, Business Week,* the *Los Angeles Times,* and others. For television and radio, I've appeared on CBS Reports, the NBC Today Show, Phil Donahue, Merv Griffin, David Susskind, and many other talk shows. I've been a writer-narrator or consultant to a whole series of documentaries on such topics as the Supreme Court, public views about civil liberties, lawyers' behavior, and, recently, employee rights issues.

Second, I've affected public awareness through speeches to a wide variety of organizations and leadership groups. On my *vita* I list some fifty-odd of these organizations just as a representative sample; in fact, they are almost too numerous to recount. Here are a few that I list as examples: the American Psychiatric Association, the Committee for Public Justice, the Alliance of American Insurers, the American Arbitration Association, the American Association for the Advancement of Science, the American Banking Association, the American Bar Association, the American Council of Life Insurance, the American Management Association, the Conference Board, the National Computer Conference, and the Public Affairs Council.

Finally, I've arranged many national seminar programs for managers of organizations over the past twenty years—for example, through the Educational Fund for Individual Rights, a nonprofit research foundation which I organized in 1979 and of which I am the president. The fund focuses on individual-employee rights in the workplace, particularly in corporate employment. The fund organized three national seminar programs on individual rights in the corporation in 1978, 1979, and 1980 and was a leader in moving those issues onto the agenda of organizational leaders, the media, etc. The fund also does basic research such as a collection of ten first-person accounts of blowing the whistle on corporate misconduct, called *Whistle Blowings: Loyalty and Dissent in the Corporation,* published in 1981, and a reader, *Individual Rights in the Corporation,* published in 1979. We have ten employees at present, and our Advisory Committee is made up of leading executives from business, labor, public-interest groups, and scholars from law and the social sciences. One of our major programs now is helping organizations to reduce employee litigation by creating strong fair-procedure systems inside.

More recently, I've established another organization called Changing Workplaces. This is an information and consulting service for business, government, and nonprofit organizations on how to manage the "people aspects" of technological change in the workplace, primarily offices, with a due regard to civil liberties and privacy. It is a way to get the results of our research projects and our policy recommendations into the decision-making cycles of organization. We've found that if organizations decide they need to pay for policy advice, you have a lot better chance of that getting adopted than if the same advice is offered free, or is just available in published materials. We have been showing how employees in office automation and also new issues of privacy need to be addressed as computers enter the organizational worlds.

There is one last way, a somewhat unusual way, in which my work has had policy effects. That is through certain individual cases of civil liberties violations that have been brought to my attention and that I've followed through on as test cases. As a result of my books, newspaper articles, and TV appearances, over the last decade or two literally hundreds of people have written to me or called me to complain that someone or some organization was violating their civil liberties. Sometimes, since I don't practice as a lawyer, I put them in touch with the appropriate lawyers or protective agencies. Of course, some of the calls I get are off the wall, from real crazies. But some have been real and terrible injustices, in which I've been able to connect people to services or groups that can help them. Such instances have also been invaluable to me as a scholar; they alert me to the problems of real people caught up in real situations, such as whistle blowing in government or business, for example. When I write an article or testify before Congress, if I can describe one or several such real cases of mistreatment or abuse, real people whose situations are compelling and will stand up under close scrutiny, that is worth oceans of passionate rhetoric in affecting policy-makers. I can think of cases where laws have been passed or regulations enacted because someone approached me, I felt the case was right, I met with the person, I documented his grievance, and then I used it (with permission, of course) as an example of some systematic abuse that I was attacking. In my congressional testimony or in my articles, I have used profiles of real people that made all the difference in the response of those I was addressing. In contrast, I think one reason

for the failure of Congress to pass a federal medical privacy law was
that the committees did not come up with real-world cases and vignettes
of people whose privacy interests as patients had been abused. Opponents of this bill said we didn't need an expensive regulation when no
one could show that real people were being hurt. Indeed, *Whistle Blowing: Loyalty Inside the Corporation* consists of ten first-person accounts
of the walking-wounded, people I met who had actually been whistle
blowers in different corporations and who had suffered for it. I wrote
an introduction and a conclusion for these ten cases, trying to show
where the problem was coming from and what might be done about it.
I had done a little writing on whistle blowing; these people came to
me, and their real cases, together with my general statements, made a
powerful statement of the problem and what might be done for it.

Because I've been concerned to have my ideas and research really
influence social policy, I've used a variety of modes to reach both decision-makers and the general public. For example, I've found it very
helpful to communicate directly with decision-makers. I did a study for
the U.S. National Bureau of Standards of how computers were being
used in health care and how rights of medical privacy were being affected. I wrote a fifteen-page executive summary of the large report of
this study and NBS sent it to every hospital administrator in the country.
Ten or twelve thousand copies of this summary were sent out by the
bureau. The summary, in brief, described what was happening in this
area, the issues of privacy it raised, and then gave twelve principles for
creating a health data system that contained the appropriate ethical and
civil liberties protections. I've heard of hundreds of hospitals that have
adopted policies based on that code. Another example comes from the
private sector. IBM asked me in 1973–75 to look at all their employee
record systems and to recommend a privacy policy for the corporation,
not only for the United States but one that IBM could apply to their
world-wide operations, adapted to different legal and social cultures.
As a result of my study, IBM promulgated a privacy code, and the IBM
model has now been distributed to and used by thousands of other organizations. IBM has announced publicly that I was their consultant for
the code so that I am not violating any confidence in relating this. In
this way, again, I have been able to influence decision-makers directly.

As I've already said, I've testified frequently before congressional
committees over three decades. I always try to come up with facts, analytic frameworks, real-life cases, and some recommendations. That approach seems to be successful with the committees. The testimony I
gave on the fair credit reporting bill before Congressman Cornelius

Gallagher's committee and Congresswoman Lenore Sullivan's committee was heavily used in the final bill that was enacted, the Fair Credit Reporting Act of 1970.

My work has also had its influence as a result of service on a number of presidential commissions. For example, I was appointed by President Nixon to the National Wiretapping Commission. It was stacked with hard conservative types, and I was added, I heard, to try to give the commission some credibility with the civil liberties community. I wound up writing a strong dissent from the report, but agreeing with some of its findings and recommendations. In addition to being a member of commissions, I've also been a consultant to such commissions as the Privacy Protection Study Commission and the United Nations Commission on Human Rights.

Many times I have briefed decision-makers orally; over the last twenty years I have spoken to top management in government agencies, corporations, professional associations, and universities. These top decision-makers usually invite such briefings. But, in addition, these people come together in settings such as the Brookings Institution seminars for top government officials, or in courses for corporation executives that many corporations conduct. I have found that there are a lot of places in our society where decision-makers and administrators and heads of advocacy groups open themselves to scholarly and activist/scholarly briefings. They don't promise to do what I recommend, but still it's a valuable way of getting ideas to these people. Also, I do this at civil liberties activist conferences.

I have already described how much newspaper and magazine writing and TV and radio talking I do; these are important media of influence on the public for new work and ideas. I guess I've talked to several hundred different professional and civic associations about my work. Knowing that my work on technology and civil liberties is relevant to their interests, values, and future, they invite me to talk to them. These modes of influence interact. The professional associations often first hear about my work from my newspaper, magazine, radio, and TV activities. Speaking to the members of professional associations is an important way to achieve change.

I think I have influence also by being a member of the peer network of civil liberties experts in a given area, such as privacy. There are about two or three dozen members of the "privacy network" who are the acknowledged experts among themselves and among outsiders as well. We talk to one another, go to meetings together, read one another's work, and counsel each other.

Since the full-time occupation that I have had for thirty years is university teaching, which serves as my primary base of location, ideas, and relationships, I would have to list my teaching and my influence on students as a primary part of my life and influence as a scholar. Former students of mine from Harvard, Yale, Cornell, and Columbia are now U.S. Senators; judges; famous lawyers; heads of companies; leaders in civil liberties, civil rights, and women's groups; leaders in publishing and the mass media; and so forth. They tell me that ideas from the classes they took with me on constitutional law and civil liberties have influenced their approach to these issues, and while this is always sweet music to a teacher's ear, I tend to think they are not just trying to make me feel good. I have always prized very highly the awards I've gotten for excellence in teaching, particularly when these came from students themselves, such as the Van Doren Prize at Columbia.

More specifically, I think there are several dozen intellectual and organizational leaders in the fields of privacy, due process, employee rights, and so forth that I consider my "protégés." Some are scholars who started their work on privacy with me and are now leading published authorities; some are constitutional law and political science experts who are now writing and teaching throughout the country; and others are organizational leaders with whom I've stayed in touch, who are putting into daily practice the kinds of policies that they worked on with me as research assistants or staff colleagues.

Of course, like any active researcher, I serve intermediary functions among researchers, foundations, activists, and all kinds of groups. People often call for information, or for advice about how to get funding, or for advice about whether a foundation should fund some application. I'm part of the rich network of information, activity, and counseling that exists in our society.

Finally, as a mode of influence, I served as the founding editor of a national journal, the *Civil Liberties Review*. I had long wanted to see something created halfway between a scholarly publication and a popular magazine, something for people who read the *New York Times* or *Harper's*. I had thought of this as long ago as when I was a young teacher at Cornell. But in the early 1970s with the support of the ACLU, and especially of its then new executive director, Aryeh Neier, I did become the director of the *Review*. We were sponsored by the publishing house of John Wiley, which hoped to make money while also helping civil liberties in the dark days of Watergate and COINTELPRO. After losing half a million dollars, first money put up by Wiley and then by the ACLU itself, the *Review* went out of business after about five years of publishing. The reason for our failure, I think, was that what had earlier been a real need for a popularly focused journal for civil liberties was now being met, in the late 1970s and today, by many general circulation newspapers and magazines, and by radio and TV. Civil liberties became a popular issue and was being well treated by the popular media. The public was getting a lot of high quality information from these other sources; they didn't need our journal any more.

As one expects, my research and ideas on civil liberties and privacy have been opposed by some people, sometimes for value reasons, sometimes for intellectual reasons, and sometimes for interest reasons. Value positions on privacy, for example, often fall into three distinct camps. There is a left position which is an activist, redistributive view arguing that we should treat privacy issues essentially in terms of enfranchising the powerless. They want to remake the institutions and power arrangements of the society. The privacy value for these people becomes part of a radical social reform position; they don't like big business, big government, or even a big society. "More privacy" is really a call for an alternative society, a critique of our fundamental institutions and social processes. Then there is the rightist position which approves of the present institutions and power arrangements. They think that there's no problem, nothing's wrong, people are not being hurt, and privacy restrictions impede the affective pursuit of valid societal and private goals. My value position is the middle one. I think that there are privacy and civil liberties dangers and abuses, that they need to be remedied, and that we can decide about the necessary changes in democratic ways. I like to suggest codes of fair information practice and privacy statutes which define the rights people have, let them know what's going on, who is making the decision, and how societal values and control can be applied. Because of my middle value position, I find myself always engaged in debate with those who say I haven't gone far enough or I've gone too far. By my advocacy, I feel I can get government or employers or insurance companies or credit granters or universities to change things in a way that more fully respects privacy and civil liberties, but I rarely advocate fundamental changes in social organization as the way to increase privacy and due process. In that sense, I am a reformist democrat.

I've had some intellectual resistance, too. There are people who criticize my work for not being theoretical or systematic enough. As I've indicated in discussing methodology, I use the method of fact-finding and eclectic use of theory, pointing to vivid cases and using surveys for collecting trend data. But my approach is not heavily quantified, and the kinds of problems I work on aren't well served by building elaborate models of behavior and trying to predict from them. I think my work is rigorous, but it doesn't start from systematic theory. This doesn't satisfy some people, those who attach greater importance to building social theory. I've also sometimes had intellectual differences with people who share my civil liberties values. For example, the facts I collected in the data banks study brought me into conflict with some civil libertarians I respect, but whose facts were just wrong about what data banks were actually being used to do, and therefore their policy prescriptions were all wrong. In another area, the ACLU has always believed in a total ban on wiretapping, as an invasion of privacy that can never be justified or controlled. I can't agree with that and have stuck by my own analysis of the necessity for some wiretapping, under limited conditions, and under tight protective safeguards.

Lastly, there has been opposition from various interest groups, for instance, from both business and labor. When I worked on race discrimination, I discovered lots of labor union discrimination against blacks and women. When I pointed out that unions were part of the system of racism, I was vehemently attacked. Some unions still oppose something I am advocating. Only one fifth of the private working force in this country is unionized today. When I say that there ought to be proper complaint and appeals systems for nonunion employees in corporations, some unions object, saying that I'm hurting their interests. They are there to organize workers and thereby protect the due process rights of employees. They feel that my recommendation for private protection systems is selling out the labor movement, which alone has the necessary power to help employees; they feel voluntary arrangements are not satisfactory. I do feel that unions play a valuable social role in protecting workers' rights. But since four fifths of Americans do not choose to belong to unions, we need other public or private mechanisms to protect those workers in their rights of expression, dissent, and process. Many unions have been hostile to the quality circle mechanisms of employee participation which I favor, because I believe in democratic participation in the workplace. The unions see some employers using quality circles for anti-union purposes, but I believe worker participation is so fundamental that I'm not willing to back away from my advocacy of it just because of some employer abuse and some union opposition.

Resistance to my work on interest grounds has come also from some corporate leaders and many federal-government executive managers who argue that people don't really care about the issue of privacy and due process rights. They claim that these are just elitist interventions into their affairs by university and civil liberties types. They feel protection of these rights is costly and unimportant. I've always tried to show these companies and agencies that people really do care, that protections are worth the costs and the disruption to their routines and interests. One part of this activity has been serving as the academic adviser to the Louis Harris organization, for the largest national public and leadership opinion survey on privacy that has been conducted, in 1979. That survey was enormously influential in documenting how broadly and deeply people care about personal and group privacy, what organizational and legal protections they want, etc. The resistance I've had from some corporations, unions, and agencies is not from all of them, of course, but at a given moment it may have been from their mainstreams. Therefore, I always look for the leading-edge organizations and institutions that, for their own interests or values, are resonating to these issues and are ready to anticipate new values and expectations by people. When I can point to these leaders as examples of sound new policies and acceptable cost levels, then the mainstream of a community or corporations or unions or government agencies will be willing to go along.

In the matter of the general relation between knowledge and social policy, I've learned that for many problems, though not all, knowledge can make a lot of difference. In many of the civil liberties areas in which I've done research, empirical knowledge is very short. In matters like censorship or public access to records, or how discrimination in employment hurts organizational effectiveness, the policy-makers operate with very little knowledge of the way things really work. If you can show them the facts, then you have enormous leverage in changing policy. I always distinguish such areas from those in which everybody knows damn well what is going on but won't change. You don't have to document the presence of racial discrimination in housing, voting, public accommodations, etc.; you have to appeal to moral values and race interests and political power to get change. So not all policy areas are fact-starved, but many are. In cases like capital punishment, for example, when social science research showed the race bias in the sentencing system, then there were grounds for change that judges could grasp. Or when research showed the gross malapportionment of voting rights of citizens, then there were grounds for legislative reappointment. When scholars and activist groups uncovered the facts about uncontrolled surveillance of citizens by the FBI and other government agencies, we helped to force the society—the courts in particular—to bring these facts into proper compliance with established norms and laws.

What I've said earlier on and what I've just said indicates my belief that it is possible to change somewhat the institutional power structure of our country. My research has brought me into touch with many of the most powerful decision-makers in our society. They exist in different spheres, in government, corporations, professional associations, universities, and advocacy groups. They are often open to change and to the application of some controls on their power. In these matters, I'm very much the pluralist. But pluralism is not a self-starting process. The degree to which a pluralist society makes progress on matters of civil liberties or justice is a function of who is trying to move the pluralist consensus forward. Advocates, movement leaders, are important. I believe we make our decisions by a consensual system among leaders of various kinds of groups. The elite studies show *leaders* of interest groups to be more liberal on civil liberties matters than *members* of their groups, and that seems correct to me. The dynamic that I'm interested in is how advocates can, at certain points and under certain conditions, push the pluralist system into changes that bring about more democracy, more equality, and more justice.

I've also learned that change is not only possible in a pluralist system but that recently change has been occurring very rapidly. Changes that used to take half centuries now take a decade; those of a decade can occur in a few years. Today, the half-life of one's education is also getting shorter. The processes of political and social life are changing so rapidly that one is both excited and confused. By the time a scholar comes up with a description of one of these processes, it may have changed and require new description. As a young man, I used to feel comfortable with cyclical theories of social change; I don't any more. We are not going back to anything much in our old world; that world will not come again. I guess I would say that by every measure we are a more egalitarian society today; we are a more justice-delivering and justice-striving society than we ever were before. Paradoxically, the new technology creates more pragmatic and discrete individualism than the old blunderbuss technologies. We treat more people today as individuals and less as members of groups. The computer allows you to customize your treatment of individuals. The flexibility of information systems permits people to take into account ten times the number of unique individual characteristics of those they are dealing with. But as we have become a more individualistic society in our lifestyles, in sexual matters, in consumer choices, and in political affiliations, we have a technology available that can, if we wish to, enhance the individual aspects of people. Overall, I think we have made our greatest advance as a society in the due process areas, the next greatest advance in equality, and the next, and it's far from negligible, in the liberty/dissent area.

Still, for the future, there's plenty of research to do and much social policy to improve. In the middle 1970s, I came to feel that issues of work were going to be one of the most important social problem issues of the 1980s and 1990s. I felt that work, as a primary social activity, was going to be transformed by new technology, by competition, and by a reordering of production and service activities. In addition, I felt that the workplace was going to be more important to all of us psychologically. As the national and international social orders became more complex, I thought, there would be more turning inward to our daily work lives, to our work relations. So I began organizing national seminars on individual rights in the corporation, on privacy rights, free expression, whistle blowing, and dissent in the workplace. Much of my research now and my planned projects for the next few years are devoted to problems in the workplace. It's a continuation of my old research and policy program, how technology is affecting work and human choices, how we might reorganize work institutions, how we might define new legal rights, new private mechanisms, new modes of compliance with rights so that litigation is reduced. How do we, in short, make private bureaucracies in the workplace more respectful to those individual rights our society wants to protect, while still advancing productivity, product and service quality, and organizational effectiveness. I continue to work on many social issues in my research, but work, technology, and individual rights are what I am mainly concerned about now.

Chapter Nine

Patterns and Conclusions

Having experienced the rich diversity and concreteness of the seven cases (or eight, if we include the prototype case in the appendix), readers may well initially feel that this diversity and concreteness transcends their capacity to fix the cases in some limited set of patterns. Although all the respondents were asked the same set of questions, they do come from different backgrounds, have different disciplinary perspectives, and speak in different "voices." The readers, too, have come with different backgrounds and perspectives and will therefore find special interest in different parts of different cases. Some of these points of special interest may well be those not directly elicited by the questions asked. To take only one example, readers who are economists might be struck by how much the discipline of economics has changed in the last forty to fifty years, as one can see in the accounts given by Ginzberg, Peck, and Pechman. Or these same readers may wonder how to settle the difference between Ginzberg's more "institutionalist" analysis of human resources and manpower problems and the more econometric approach embodied in Gary Becker's use of the concept of "human capital." Both sociologists and economists might be interested in Coleman's report that his analysis of school desegregation and differential school performance was criticized and differently explained by economists. And, to take one final instance from the same realm of social science, sociologists might wonder how to cope with Rossi's statement that his use of microeconomic as well as sociological analysis in his study of recidivism among released prisoners was resisted by "hard-line" sociological criminologists. Like all oral histories, the value of the cases is not exhausted by the answers to the questions explicitly put to them. Oral histories may produce special and unintended stimulation for each reader.

Still, our main and common interest as social scientists in these cases is in the patterns they may show about the relation between empirical social research and social policy. Can the cases give more solid grounding to the insights of others who have addressed themselves to this matter, mostly in passing rather than through intensive research or the kind of detailed cases we have collected here? Do they call for different questions, more specified questions, better research methods, and better analysis? The patterns that the cases reveal are not, of course, to be taken as final and complete. They are steps along the way to still better understanding. They should be construed mostly as general guides or, sometimes, more specific hypotheses, for further research. Such research, certainly, would profit from a series of highly focused studies, bearing on each of our many questions; it would profit from larger samples; it would profit from more explicitly comparative materials. This book should be seen as a beginning, not an end.

Our search for patterns will be divided into two parts in this chapter: first, some general points that have emerged from this research and from the cases; second, some patterns that have been elicited directly by the questions asked, together with attempts to explain or speculate about those patterns in ways that go a little beyond the rationales for the questions presented in chapter 1.

Some General Points

The Effectiveness of Social Research for Social Policy

The cases presented here, chosen for that purpose, to be sure, give evidence of the fact that social science research can be effective, at least under the conditions described in the patterns reported below. The cases are to be taken only as evidence, not final proof; but an extreme view of the ineffectiveness of social science research, it would now seem, is untenable. Contrariwise, our evidence is no demonstration that social research is always effective. The cases, as illustrations of some kinds of effectiveness, should be useful to the policy- or decision-maker who wants to know whether and how some social research might be effective. The cases also illustrate that research may develop potentials for policy effectiveness even though the researcher did not so intend. For social scientists, the cases may help them to convince potential funders who have policy interests that their science and craft may be of use. And, of course, the cases will provide to sociologists of science the beginnings of still better understanding of the nature and processes of effectiveness of social research for decision-making and policy-making.

"Quiet Cases"

Except for Coleman, all the cases are what we called, in chapter 1, quiet cases; that is, they are not highly visible in wide sectors of the social science and public policy communities. A likely generalization from our cases is that most cases of social science effectiveness will be quiet cases, known only to some set of subspecialists in the social sciences who attend largely to their own work and that of their peers. Scientific workers are only in the very largest sense a single community. Instead, the work of science is done in many small communities, sometimes overlapping in significant ways, but mostly focusing on the problems immediately at hand. The Coleman case became so highly visible and widely known in the social science community and in the broader public community for the following special set of reasons. His first study was directly mandated by congressional legislation, the Civil Rights Act of 1964. This study was a triumphant symbol of usefulness for the social science community at large and was so noted. Coleman became a rare social scientist member of the President's Scientific Advisory Board, a group highly visible to the general science community. He was seen in photos consulting with President Nixon about his work. Most important, perhaps, was the nature of the policy issues his work addressed. Desegregation, civil rights, school equality, the possibility of support for religious and private schools—all of these were burning national policy and moral issues. Coleman's work stirred up a storm of scientific discussion and moral controversy. Some of his former students even, as well as others, turned against him on grounds of both methodology and morality. His research became a focus of acrimonious discussion in the highest councils of the American Sociological Association and at its annual meeting. Altogether, his has been a most unusual case and it would seem that cases of this degree of visibility are likely to occur only infrequently. Only when there are a great many such individual "quiet cases" seen as an aggregate will the effectiveness of social science become more clearly visible and then come to be as much taken for granted as is the effectiveness and usefulness of natural science. There are degrees of relative visibility or quietness in all science, but mostly it is relatively quietly effective.

Similarities Between Natural and Social Science

Comparison of the relative effectiveness of natural and social science suggests the desirability of looking more generally for possible similarities between them in their actual and perceived effectiveness and in the ways in which such effectiveness is achieved. Like those in the social sciences, most of the cases of effectiveness in the natural sciences are also quiet ones. The highly visible technological breakthroughs in the natural sciences are composed of many smaller developments usually, aggregated in an incremental way to produce the final highly visible effects. Such big breakthroughs in the natural sciences may be no more frequent, proportionally, than is the case for the social sciences, although of course in absolute numbers both the visible and the quiet cases are very much larger than they are in the social sciences.

There are further apparent similarities between the natural and social sciences. Our cases show that there is no simple determinism of policy and social consequences by research knowledge; knowledge has its effectiveness in conjunction with other factors, as is illustrated, again, by the Coleman case. If the strong moral and political commitment of the civil rights activities had not taken his findings to court, these findings would not have had the effectiveness they did. Just so, there is no simple knowledge or technological determinism in the natural sciences. For example, it's not just the great increase in the power of biomedical knowledge and technology that has so greatly increased public concern for medical ethics. To produce this increased concern and activity, new medical technology has interacted with the greatly increased communication and discussion of the significance of that technology in all the media, with the increased call for more equity and equality in our society, and, finally, with the heightened moral sensitivity that has recently spread not only among professional philosophers but in the general public as well.[1]

---

[1] Bernard Barber, "Renaissance and transformation in medical ethics," unpublished, Symposium: Perspectives on Medical Ethics, Allegheny College, May 1987.

Many other examples of possibly similar conditions for the effectiveness of natural and social science could be suggested, but that is not our task here. It is perhaps enough for now to note these possible similarities and look for them as we seek to understand the nature of social science effectiveness. This is to say that any good sociology of social science will pay close attention to the sociology of natural science.

The Importance of Washington

Our national capital, Washington, is an important place in every case in this book. It is perhaps not surprising, given that in the American political system Washington is most often, as Pechman says in connection with taxation policy, "where the action is." Compared with state and city governments, Washington has been, by far, the largest funder and user of social science research and advice. What is remarkable is the wide variety of social science activities and functions that Washington has provided for our respondents. They have served on committees and commissions and as staff in executive agencies and legislative groups. They have testified before congressional committees and national commissions. They have briefed administrators and their advisory staffs. They have brought knowledge to Washington, but Washington has given them experience with policy problems that has, in turn, affected their research. The openness of Washington to social researchers has been a great advantage to the development of social science. The fact that American social science is not a "closet science," not just a "science of the chair," is due in part to Washington's considerable receptivity. Social researchers do not play the very large and direct role in government policy and decision-making that their counterparts in the Scandinavian countries are alleged to play, but they have their place and function. This place and function varies somewhat by which party is in power and which political ideology prevails, but no government now finds it possible to do without social scientists' research and policy advice.

The Importance of Research Organizations

Like the natural sciences, the social sciences have their "little science" and their "big science."[2] Although there remain many "little science" individual researchers in the social sciences, increasingly, as the ever-

---

[2] Derek J. de Solla Price, *Little Science, Big Science . . . And Beyond* (New York: Columbia University Press, 1986).

larger number of multi-authored articles in the professional journals show, there is more and more collaborative research. In some cases, and this started as early as the 1920s with the National Bureau of Economic Research founded by Wesley Clair Mitchell, research has been found to be best carried on in well-organized and continuing research organizations. Our cases report the considerable importance of these large research organizations. The Brookings Institution, especially populated by political scientists and economists, was indispensable for the continuing program of research and policy activities on the subject of national taxation policy of Joseph Pechman. Coleman says that the part of his research that used large-scale statitistical and survey data would have been impossible without the facilities of the National Opinion Research Center at the University of Chicago. It is interesting to note that one of the uses of these large and continuing research organizations is that they can provide able research assistants and apprentices—either graduate students, in the case of a university-based organization like NORC, or interns, in the case of a free-standing organization like Brookings.

In some of our cases, the researcher found he had to set up his own large and continuing research organization. Ginzberg's Conservation of Human Resources group at Columbia University has been essential for his continuing program of research over the last thirty years. There has been turnover in the staff, but the organization persists. Westin, too, reports that he has set up special research organizations for various projects that continue over a span of time.

Despite its considerable receptivity to social research, official Washington has remained ambivalent about establishing large-scale research organizations. On the positive side, Congress has established the Congressional Budget Office, which has achieved a good reputation for impartial economic research and advice and which has been a valuable training ground in the research and policy process for generations of academic economists who have sought out opportunities to spend some time at the CBO while retaining their permanent location in university and college positions. Invaluable, in addition, are such large collectors of social data as the monthly Current Population Survey (over 50,000 households surveyed) and the monthly price surveys of the Bureau of Labor Statistics. Also on the positive side are various small staff research groups in various executive agencies such as the Treasury and Commerce Departments. Even in research groups which are primarily devoted to the natural sciences, such as the National Institutes of Health and the Office of Technology Assessment, some social researchers have their established places.

On the negative side, Washington has never set up a multi-topic, multi-policy opinion survey research organization to match the quality of facilities it provides in the physical and biological sciences. Survey research of this kind remains restricted to the private and university sectors. Actually, the NORC is the only university-based multi-topic survey research organization, since such organizations require considerable funding. Only the commercial organizations in the private sector can afford to run permanent survey research facilities. Both government policy and social science research would probably be advanced by the establishment of a general survey research facility that is the counterpart to an organization like the Congressional Budget Office.

Patterns Elicited by Our Questions

Early Training

As hypothesized in our questions about the significance of early training on the style as well as the substance of their work and careers, the respondents affirm its considerable importance. Graduate instructors in all cases, and even undergraduate instructors in some cases, are mentioned as important teachers, mentors, and role models. In recent years, feminist scholars have made much of the importance of mentors as powerful agents in advancing the careers of their favored students. The feminists have asserted that male professors have been unwilling to become mentors to female students, thus putting such students at a career disadvantage. Most of this discussion has centered on the powerful role of the male professor in obtaining jobs for his students. There has been little attention paid to the other functions of mentors, as teachers and role models. Indeed, there has been more ideological expression than systematic research and analysis on the functions of mentors. Research is needed to sort out the different and possibly multiple functions that mentors can play.

Some of our respondents mention influential instructors primarily as teachers. Westin, for example, names three teachers who influenced him both intellectually and morally at the Harvard Law School and three also in the Harvard Department of Political Science, where he took a Ph.D. after taking his LL.B. at the Law School. But Westin also indicates that one of his graduate teachers was a role model as well: Paul Cherington had already, as Westin hoped to, combined law and political science. Peck also mentions a role model when he speaks of the dramatic effect on him when his teacher, the distinguished economist and government adviser Edward S. Mason refused to take a telephone call from the President of the United States while he was teaching a class. Janowitz points to still another function of mentors. As an under-graduate, coming to know and admire the political scientist Harold Lass-well, he was aware that Lasswell was a kind of "talent scout," as he calls him, for social science. Lasswell sought to recruit Janowitz not only to graduate training in social science but to the University of Chicago par-ticularly.

Undergraduate teachers as mentors are most likely to have this "tal-ent scout" function. Peck mentions a political scientist teacher at Ober-lin College, reminding us what a crucial role the small liberal arts col-lege and its teachers have played in recruiting bright students to go on to graduate training in the teacher's field and often in his or her univer-sity of origin. Over many years, about a dozen of such small men's and women's undergraduate liberal arts colleges have had teachers who, as mentors, have been prolific in training future academics. Perhaps the most striking case was a physics teacher at Reed College in Portland, Oregon. As a result of his teaching and guidance, so many of his under-graduate students had gone on to graduate training and successful aca-demic careers in that field that the American Physics Society presented him with a special medal and a cash award.

Although none of our respondents specifically mentions the first-job and subsequent career help of their influential teachers and mentors, there is no question that such help is rendered both formally and infor-mally. Mentors praise their students orally in informal intercourse with peers at other colleges and universities and they write strong letters of recommendation. This, too, is a matter that all professionals recognize but has not been systematically researched. Still, the cases show that the other mentoring functions, those of being role models, of encouraging styles and kinds of work, more theoretical or more applied and policy-oriented, are also important.

This is not to say that mentors are solely responsibile for the direc-tion that students, undergraduate and graduate, may take. Pechman mentions the influence, in his undergraduate days, of his awareness of family and general poverty, along with discussions with fellow students at City College in New York of democracy, socialism, and communism, in turning him to concern for social problems and their amelioration.

The reports about their early training from our respondents point to another pattern and another area of needed research. Past discussion of such training has tended to focus on instructors as mentors, not on the strong influence of fellow graduate students. Peck in economics at

Harvard, Pechman in economics at Wisconsin, and Janowitz in sociology
at Chicago mention the "strong" cohort of fellow graduate students.
What are the intellectual and moral functions of fellow graduate students, especially "strong" ones? We know that one of the additional
strengths of graduate departments with outstanding teacher-researchers
is their attractiveness to potentially outstanding graduate students. In
her study of Nobel Prize winners, Zuckerman has documented the fact
that potential winners often have studied with actual winners. As aggre-
gates of "strong" students gather in particular academic departments, in
both the natural and social sciences, what functions do they have for
one another? How do they affect one another's knowledge, style, and
commitment to applied or theoretical work? If our questions on early
training had included some questions on fellow graduate students, all of
our respondents might have had statements to make. It would be worth
asking such questions in further research that seeks to get a more complete picture of the effects of early training on not only the intellectual
substance but also the moral and policy research commitments of social
science researchers.

Finally, it should be noted that the molding of social researchers
does not stop with their early training. Other important influences may
supervene at later stages of a career. I reported the important influence,
during my first university job after leaving graduate school, of my colleague Paul Lazarsfeld. As against the more theoretically oriented training I had received at Harvard, Larzarsfeld taught me the importance and
techniques of empirical research. And Coleman mentions that even as a
mature researcher he profited not only from the special enthusiasm and
hard work of his graduate students and research assistants but from
their "new ideas." The very important influences of early training are
supplemented by new influences that may extend throughout the active
researcher's career. To use a phrase that is now quite popular in the
study of individual lives and careers, the whole "life course" of the researcher will repay careful study and analysis.

Sources of Empirical Research Interests: Values, Theory, Methodology, Policy

One of the long-standing controversies in social science has centered
on the question of whether value-free social science is possible. An
extreme "positivistic" view of science has held that the theories and
methodologies of science isolate it from any "contamination" by values.
Science is objective, this view holds, and only the values of science it-

self, enjoining objectivity in the form of methodological purity and critical skepticism, are legitimate for scientists. At the other extreme, the
"interpretative" or "social construction of reality" view has held that the
activities and the very substance of science are shaped by the nonscientific values and interests of the working scientist, even if he is not aware
of this shaping. There is no such thing, this view holds, as value-free
social or even natural science.

It would seem that a more interactionist or interdependence assumption about the relations among values, theory, and methodology may be
more useful. On this assumption, each of these factors has some measure of independence, not always very clear in any given case, but each
factor is also always interdependent. This interdependence assumption
makes it possible to recognize the role that the "interpretative" school
claims for values and the role that the "positivistic" school claims for
theory and methodology, while still preserving for science its measure
of objectivity in its accounts of the natural and social worlds.

While none of our respondents makes this interdependence assumption explicit, it is what they all seem to hold. Although they initially emphasize one or another of the factors of theory, values, and methodology as guides to their research, they indicate that they soon see the
necessary importance of the others. Their emphasis on one or another
of these factors may vary from one piece of work to another or at different phases of their career. Moreover, they may see all three factors,
as Ginzberg says explicitly, as "intertwined."

As working scientists, not philosophers of science, the respondents
seem not to have been very much concerned about the different roles
of values, theory, and methodology. Westin does say that he was primarily concerned for civil rights and equality values and was eclectic and
interdisciplinary in his use of theory and methods. Do most working
scientists take this kind of matter-of-fact view of the relations among
values, theory, and methodology? Is this better or worse for the advancement of social science? What role does explicit philosophy of science have in the actual working of science? Does it influence working
scientists, and if so how? Certainly many modern social scientists have
been concerned about questions of philosophy of science, but we do
not know how their concerns have affected working research scientists.

Although they probably thought of their research as quite objective
in its theory and methodology, none of the researchers hesitated to
affirm strongly the importance of their values. As might be expected
from a group of American social researchers, among whom survey data
show the predominance of liberal social values, our researchers are

most likely to say that their chief value was that of equality, sometimes formulated as pure equality, more often expressed as equality of opportunity, and sometimes as equity, in which equality bows a little to the value of justice. A strong secondary value, again not unexpected in modern America because of the importance it attaches to the general value of rationality, is efficiency. The efficiency value is especially important for the economists, because of their theoretical assumption of market rationality. And economists, recognizing their dual moral commitment to equality and efficiency, acknowledge the necessity of "trade-offs," or the problem of balancing equality and efficiency against one another. Pechman specifically refers to the classic discussion of trade-offs between equality and efficiency by his late Brookings colleague, the economist Arthur Okun.

Some of our respondents do not think merely of the balancing among values or among theory, values, and research but of the positive functions that interaction among them may have. Coleman, for example, started out in his research wanting to prove the general usefulness of social research for social policy. He admits to a strong disciplinary motivation; he wanted to improve the standing of social research by demonstrating its usefulness. As he became more and more interested in policy research, however, he came to feel that his research was valuable for improving his ability as a theorist. It made him try to theorize more explicitly and more powerfully about the macrostructure of society; in his most recent work he has devoted himself intensively to this theoretical task. Moreover, as a result of his experience with moral critics of his work, Coleman has come to see the possible function of value conflicts for improving the theoretical and methodological aspects of social research. Value challenges may focus one's mind ever more sharply on the theory and method of one's work and permit one to see possible weaknesses and improvements one did not see originally. Coleman's emerging views about the potentially fruitful relations among values, theory, methodology, and social policy are not unique among social researchers.

Does the balancing that our respondents do among values and among theory and research come without cost? Do they not in their various roles as moralists, theorists, methodologists, and policy researchers, do our researchers not experience what sociologists refer to as "role strains," the social and psychological difficulties that occur sometimes in the endless balancing that all social action may involve? To investigate this general problem, the respondents were asked if they had become social activists as well as social researchers and whether having these two roles involved "role strain" between social activism and social and policy research. Indeed, as we have just seen in Coleman's case, instead of "role strain" we may sometimes get what we may call "role synergism," in which potentially conflicting roles may actually be useful for each other. This "role synergism" is quite clear in Westin's research and activism on civil liberties and privacy policy. By joining activist organizations, partly as a participant observer or researcher to be sure, but partly also out of value commitment, Westin felt he was able more successfully to discern emerging policy issues and have access to the developing information and data that these activist agencies have to collect and confront. This possibility may not be open to all researchers, for lack of the requisite activist organizations or because of personal distaste for or lack of skill in an activist capacity. When they are available, however, it would seem to be desirable to follow Westin's example. Among social scientists, our cases show, it may presently be somewhat easier for economists to become activists because so many government, private, and voluntary sector activist organizations now define it as desirable to have economists as policy-committed members and consultants. There is probably a measure of welcome on the activist front for economists which does not now exist on the whole for sociologists and political scientists. As the policy relevance of the research of the latter increases, however, their welcome as useful members of activist organizations is likely to increase.

The Influence of Sponsors

Science, of course, has no supporting resources of its own. It always depends on financial and moral support from its environing social system. This dependence raises problems for science. Ideally, to preserve its autonomy, science would like support with no value or interest strings attached. Some scientists have indeed made claims for such wholly disinterested social support, on the grounds that pure science is such an important value that it deserves support entirely on its own terms. Most scientists, however, acknowledging the reality of the separate values and interests of the rest of society, have grounded their claims for support in the appeal to social usefulness. Still, even on this ground, scientists seek to preserve as much of their autonomy as possible.

How did our respondents get sponsors and support? How did they preserve the necessary degree of autonomy? In a number of different ways, it would seem.

Sometimes, the programmatic values and interest of sponsors in gov-

ernment, foundations, voluntary nonprofit organizations, and corporations overlapped with those of the researcher and so their support was
not felt to be restrictive. The government support that Coleman and
Rossi got for their research came from programs that conformed to
their own values and so was acceptable. Indeed, in Rossi's case, Howard
Rosen, the government program officer for his program, was so helpful
with not only financial but also intellectual and moral support that Rossi
eventually dedicated the book reporting his research to Rosen. In
Janowitz's research on the military, specific foundation programs were
essential sponsors. When the Ford Foundation had a program supporting basic social research and the Russell Sage Foundation had a program to communicate the findings of social research to professions
such as medicine, law, and the military, Janowitz's research profited
from them.

In Europe, in countries like France, Germany, and Britain, the government has tended to be far and away the largest sponsor of research
in the natural and social sciences. The United States has been different. Although the government is enormously important here, chiefly
through the National Science Foundation and the National Institutes of
Health, the United States has had a more pluralistic system for the support of science. Our researchers have had support from all sectors of
this pluralistic system: not only from government, but from foundations,
trade associations, corporations, and voluntary associations. This pluralistic system often makes it possible for social research to have several
opportunities for sponsorship; it enables social research to look for support where it would pinch the least. Complete autonomy is not always
possible, of course, but alternative sources of sponsorship can reduce
the likelihood of undue influence on theory, methods, findings, and
policy recommendations.

Research support comes in forms other than the financial. Westin reports essential aid in the form of access to data from corporations,
nonprofit voluntary organizations, and professional and trade associations. Both Westin and Ginzberg mention the legitimacy and intellectual
support that are provided by advisory panels set up by them for their
research projects. When the research involved controversial topics, such
as invasion of workers' privacy by corporations using computerized
data, Westin put representatives of both the corporations and their ad-
versaries on his panel. Such advisory panels were a way of trying to balance diverse beliefs, values, and interests. An additional advantage of
this approach was that it made it easier often to get support from funding agencies anxious to avoid charges of partisanship.

Not all research sponsorship and support is welcome. Because of the ideological objections of his liberal, antimilitary colleagues and students in the university, Janowitz refused to ask for research support from the Department of Defense. His support came instead from the presumably less evil programs of the foundations. Janowitz wanted the legitimacy that approval of his colleagues and students could give him. He felt he could not trade off this legitimacy for the financial support of the Department of Defense. Because of the presence of so many value and interest conflicts in society and in potential funding sponsors, social researchers may frequently face difficult decisions about balancing off different kinds of support that they need for their work.

Main and Unexpected Findings

In addition to tending to proclaim science as "value-free," the positivistic view of science tended to exaggerate the degree to which scientific work and findings are planned and predictable. Extending as far back as the nineteenth century, there were aperçus to the contrary, such as Pasteur's remark, "Chance favors the prepared mind," but general doctrine had it that there was little of the unexpected or chanciness about science. Recent sociology of science writing and research have corrected the older belief. Unexpected findings and happy "accidental" discoveries (or serendipity, as such discoveries have come to be called, using the term coined by Horace Walpole in the eighteenth century) are now defined as a standard part of scientific work. Sociology of science research now seeks to specify more satisfactorily what unexpectedness and chance mean and the conditions under which they occur.

Our cases provide some clues to this improved meaning and better understanding. The cases reveal that established scientific or commonsense assumptions, especially when they are ideologically based, may lead to expectations that are falsified by careful research. One of the clearest examples is given in Westin's case. Out of value and associated ideological assumptions about the importance of individual rights to privacy, in his first, nonresearch book on the subject Westin asserted that the very existence of computers resulted in corporate and governmental invasion of workers' and citizens' privacy. However, when Westin did actual research on 55 governmental and corporate agencies and firms, he discovered no such invasion of privacy. Westin was then able to specify the various constraints on invasion of privacy practices that existed within the corporations and in the society at large. Westin had transformed what "everybody," at least of a certain ideological persuasion, "knew" into unexpected fact. Westin did not go on to assert that computers could not, under any conditions, intrude on valued privacy but only that they did not under the conditions then prevailing in his 55 research sites. Westin says his finding transformed him from a "technological determinist" to a "soft determinist." Such determinism is a multifactor social determinism.

Ginzberg's case shows how basic theoretical assumptions may be wrong or only partially correct and be overturned or qualified by a long-time program of research. Ginzberg started his research on manpower and human resources policy with psychological, individualistic theoretical assumptions: individuals, both workers and managers, were responsible for wasted manpower resources. Over the course of much research, he came to change his basic theoretical assumptions. Research showed him that system and structural determinants were basic for the use of human resources.

Pechman's finding that not only the rich but everybody profited in some measure from tax loopholes seems to have been unexpected partly because of contrary commonsense assumptions and partly because of his liberal values. This unexpected finding made him realize how difficult it was going to be to reform American tax policy so as to include in what he called "comprehensive income tax" *all* income, excluding nothing.

Finally, contrary to his initial assumptions about the determinants of racial segregation in the schools, Coleman found the unexpected: greater within-district segregation was accompanied by greater between-district desegregation. Searching for an explanation other than psychological prejudice, Coleman formulated his theory of "white flight."

Empirical social research, like natural science research, through unexpected and chancy findings, can challenge commonsense, ideological, and theoretical assumptions. The new findings are not always accepted, of course, nor do they necessarily change social policy. But they have the potential, if accepted, to do so and are an important function of careful empirical social research.

Effectiveness

As hypothesized in the questions addressed to all the respondents, the effectiveness of their research and policy activities was realized in a variety of ways. Their research affected public "consciousness," that is, public knowledge and values on certain social problems; they themselves framed (as Westin did), or made inputs into, legislation; they in-

fluenced the decisions of governmental organizations and private corporations, helped to educate powerful elites, and saw their work cited in
decisions of the courts. In some cases, an individual social researcher
had several of these kinds of effects. Westin, probably because he was a
self-conscious activist as well as researcher, a person who wanted to see
policy reformed and was willing to work at the task, had every one of
these kinds of effects on civil rights and privacy policy. He was a determined, competent, innovative activist in communicating his findings and
policy recommendations. Such a stance undoubtedly increases effectiveness. Pechman, too, welcomed a variety of kinds of opportunities for
policy effectiveness. He wrote articles for the public press, gave congressional testimony, and briefed presidential candidate and then President Carter. The desire to be policy-effective and the willingness to
work at realizing this wish is undoubtedly important for success. Other
favorable conditions, as we shall see in a little while, are of course also
essential.

The researcher's style in seeking effectiveness varies among our cases
and makes a difference in the degree of success achieved. Rossi, for
example, declaring himself to be generally skeptical of his own and
others' researches and findings, says he has to proclaim all the qualifications he feels about his work. In dealings with agency staffs and Congress, this has made him a less effective advocate of his recommendations. Pechman, in contrast, reports that he knows that the decision-
makers and congressional committees want "straight" answers. In all his
statements about tax policy, therefore, he says, he does not waffle or
give qualifications. Westin's style goes one step beyond "straight" answers. In addition, he always tries to make his case vivid and convincing
by presenting real concrete cases of the abuses and problems he is discussing. Talking about specific real-life people and organizations, he
feels, increases his effectiveness.

Janowitz's experience illustrates a mode of effectiveness not directly
inquired after in the cases but which may underlie and be interwoven
with the kinds of effectiveness we did ask about. Janowitz stresses that
his research, and that of the numerous colleagues he eventually got to
join him in the field of military research, changed the ways of thinking,
the self-conceptions, that the military had. Military policy-makers had to
address the questions his research turned up, even when they didn't
give the same answers finally. His new ways of stating military manpower and military policy problems, as embodied in such new concepts
as "citizen-soldiers" and "constabulary force," concepts that students in
all professional military training schools had to confront when they did

required reading in his book and articles, had both indirect and direct effects in actual military practice.

Clearly there are many ways for empirical social research to become effective in social policy. This is especially so when the researcher tries competently and with the right style to be effective and when favorable social, political, and economic conditions make it possible for his efforts to succeed. Effectiveness often has to be "prompted" in the face of ignorance and resistance. We need research on the willingness and aptitudes of social researchers for this often necessary "promotion" of their research.

Modes of Influence

Although the answers of our respondents to questions about types of effectiveness inevitably overlapped somewhat with their answers on modes of influence, some different patterns emerge. The researchers, for one thing, seem to have been following the rule established in communication research that it is desirable to send out the same message several times in different channels. The researchers often used as many channels as were available to them: books, professional and general articles, TV, radio, addresses to professional associations, testimony to national commissions and congressional committees—in short all the channels of communication and influence hypothesized in the list of questions.

The researchers also seemed to know that all channels and all audiences are not the same at all times for all purposes. For example, when first defining a social situation as a social problem, Ginzberg, and Westin, too, found that books and general periodical reviews were the modes of influence best suited to raising public consciousness. In his book, Rossi explicitly addressed different types of communication audience. He reports that he deliberately divided the book into three sections: the first chapter was an "executive summary," written for busy decision-makers presumed to have scarce time for reading; another section, consisting of several chapters, was written for the "intelligent layman"; and the last chapters were written for his theoretically and technically competent peers. Westin, when he was trying to promote a new hospital privacy code, sent some ten to twelve thousand summaries of his studies on the subject to the hospital administrators all over the country who would be in charge of composing and promulgating such codes. Janowitz, in order to reach his social researcher peers and attentive military elites, and Westin, to reach the general public, started journals in, respectively, military sociology and civil rights news and issues. Thus, the researchers showed considerable knowledge and skill in targeting their findings and policy recommendations to the right audience at the right time.

One of the patterns of communication influence that appears in my case is the way in which the media interact with one another, often to heighten the researcher's influence. My book was favorably reviewed in *Science*, which is widely read by working scientists, both natural and social. But it was not noticed in general journals like the *New York Times*. However, when a summary of the book appeared as an article in *Scientific American*, a much more general and less technical publication than *Science*, this article became news for the *New York Times*, which then published an article reporting my findings. TV and radio stations in New York also responded to this *media interaction effect*. The media pay attention to one another. A researcher's influence can be magnified in this way.[3]

Despite the evidence that the media are often important modes of influence, the researchers' different styles and personalities gave them different views of the usefulness of media influence. As a result of his almost twenty years of experience with the media, Coleman thinks that there has been a great increase in attention paid to the problems of public education. But he also thinks that this attention has led to the "gross simplification" of his findings; he finds the media "extraordinarily unsuited to the complexities of social research results." Perhaps this is because, as Coleman acknowledges in regard to TV, he feels uneasy in TV appearances. Ginzberg shares this uneasiness with TV but not, apparently, with the other news media. Simplification, as Jonathan Cole has shown in research on how the risks of hypercholesterolemia are reported in the press, surely does occur in news reports of research findings. But sometimes simplification makes a point with great clarity. For example, Peck reports that the article by a group of Yale Law School students showing that airline fares in California, where there was no intrastate government regulation, were cheaper per mile than in U.S. interstate airline traffic, which was regulated by the Civil Aeronautics Board, was widely reported in the general press and seems to have had a larger influence than more technical books and articles on airline and other transportation deregulation.

Influence through social networks is quintessentially evident in

---

[3] On the media and science, see Dorothy Nelkin, *Selling Science* (New York: W.H. Freeman, 1987).

Janowitz's case, where not only the formal instruments of a journal and professional meetings but also informal conversations put Janowitz at the very center of an ever-enlarging network of researchers and policy advisers. Janowitz reports that he set aside regular times to be in his office to receive calls from members of his network, which was largely a research network. In contrast, Ginzberg describes the importance of a network of elite decision-makers in the government and in corporations, indeed, eventually around the world. Pechman, in Washington where "the action" on taxation policy was for both research and policy, found that city a strategic site for important network influence.

For the world of influence, as for the world of social research funding, the situation is pluralistic. The pluralistic economy of funding has as it counterpart and environment a pluralistic social system of influence. In American society, as they seek policy effectiveness for their research, our respondents pushed at many different points of the pluralistic social system where influence could be wielded.

Resistance

Just because the social system and the points of influence, therefore, are pluralistic, and because a social system is composed of a complex set of values and of intellectual, political, and economic "interests," there is also often one or another kind of resistance to the social researcher's findings and policy recommendations. Not all of the different parts of the pluralistic social system are favorable in general, or favorable at any given time, to social research findings and the policy recommendations based thereon. It is clear that social science knowledge must expect that its facts and policy recommendations have to compete with a variety of other knowledge, moral, and interest factors as it seeks policy effectiveness. What the neutral social system analyst calls the "competition" or "interaction" among these several factors may look like biased "resistance" to the social science researcher seeking to have his ideas enacted into social policy. Whether it is called "competition" or "resistance," the social researcher can only sometimes expect to have his ideas wholly unopposed on some important moral, interest, or intellectual ground. When the social researcher is recommending policy, he is thereby in politics, whether he acknowledges it or not, and he must remember what Max Weber said, "Politics is the slow boring of hard boards."

There are many examples of resistance in our cases. One of the clearest examples is provided by Pechman. When he discovered that nearly every segment of the society profited from tax loopholes, and when he recommended as tax policy that all of these loopholes be removed, he experienced resistance from a wide variety of value and interest groups: the aged, business, labor, homeowners, the medical profession, philanthropic and nonprofit voluntary organizations dependent on tax-deductible gifts, and many others. When congressional committees in 1986 were trying to enact a new tax bill approximating Pechman's long-recommended "comprehensive income tax," the media were filled with stories and pictures of the hundreds of lobbyists representing all the different value and interest groups that were seeking to preserve their exemptions and loopholes.

There is another clear example in my case. My research finding that the human subjects of biomedical research were sometimes abused, and my recommendation that there be government regulation of such experimentation, met with both indifference and hostility from the biomedical research profession. The absolutistic value they placed on their own professional autonomy resisted a policy of even relatively mild outside control such as was proposed by me and which had been mandated by the National Institutes of Health because of its fear of lawsuits. Another example is in Ginzberg's report that the preconceived and somewhat rigid ideas of military leaders about the level of quality they required in recruits made them resistant to his evidence that what the military defined as "low quality" recruits could be successfully trained and used.

It should be made explicit that competition or, as the researcher himself may define it, "resistance" is not necessarily intellectually or morally wrong. Social systems proceed through the interaction, competition, and frequent conflict of their different parts. The social researcher's right may be someone else's wrong. And, as the case of Coleman shows, rights and wrongs do not occur only between those inside and outside the social research community. Coleman's right was defined as wrong on intellectual and moral grounds by some of his fellow social scientists—indeed, in at least one case, by one of his former students and colleagues.

General Conditions of Policy Effectiveness

Toward the end of their interviews, our respondents were asked to reflect in general on what their research and policy experience had taught them about the effectiveness of research and about the processes of social power and social change. Do any patterns appear in their answers? Some do, but before reporting them it is important to describe some essential characteristics of our sample of respondents and how those characteristics may have affected their answers. First, our cases are all instances of success, of actual effectiveness; indeed, they were selected for their success. A sample of failures might have had different views on the possibilities for effectiveness and on the processes of social power and social change. Still, further research would do well to include failed cases.

Second, all of our cases were older, liberal products of the 1930s, 1940s, and 1950s. The cohorts of social scientists of those times were predominantly liberal and believers in social and political pluralism and in the possibilities of social change. Although most social scientists probably are still of this liberal persuasion, there is now a set of social scientists and social researchers, products of the 1960s youth and ideological rebellion, who think of themselves as radical and revolutionary. This is, as Immanuel Wallerstein has recently written, "the era of a thousand Marxisms," and the new, if probably still minority, cohort of social scientists believes in capitalist monopoly of power and in the need for revolutionary rather than gradual, incrementalist processes of social and political power. Further research would do well, also, to include these dissenting social scientists in its sample.

Because of their success, then, in influencing social policy, all our respondents believe in the effectiveness of empirical social research. But not all by itself and not under all conditions. In my case, it seems clear that my findings would not have had the influence they did have on policy for the regulation of biomedical research if it had not been for the great political and moral force of Senator Kennedy in the civil rights field. Kennedy cared about civil rights, he cared especially about such civil rights for blacks, and he had a strong concern for medical problems. As the chairman of the Senate Subcommittee on Health he was able to translate his concerns for these matters, after the Tuskegee scandal had aroused general public consciousness, into legislation setting up the National (later President's) Commission for the Protection of the Human Subjects of Biomedical and Behavioral Research. It was in the context of Senator Kennedy's moral and political power that my testimony on findings and policy had its influence.

In his answer, Ginzberg gives a more general and therefore vaguer account of the conditions leading to effectiveness. Congressional choices, he says, are determined by the "existing political situation." He feels that no matter what the knowledge base on any problem, not everything is possible at any given time. This is so, further, because there is often a range of academic views on major social and political issues. Congress and its committee staffs can pick and choose among the different social science views in the light of the existing political situation. Obviously it is a task for social research not only to investigate and specify the particulars of any given political situation but to seek to generalize the conditions under which effectiveness occurs.

One generalization that our researchers do seem to agree on with respect to effectiveness is that knowledge is only one part of the political process. They put this point in different ways. Janowitz says that social research is a staff and not a line function; social researchers are not decision-makers. Janowitz recommends that social scientists recommending policy use what he calls the "enlightenment model." Rossi concurs. Although acknowledging that he had originally thought that the social researcher as the technical expert should tell the decision-maker what to do, he has come to feel strongly that knowledge is only one part of the political process. He feels that social scientists sharpen and clarify issues, not determine outcome. Even Westin, whose research has been very effective in the field of civil rights, says that while knowledge can make a lot of difference, this is not always so. Sometimes people know the facts but won't change their values, and he instances the sentiments and legislation for capital punishment. Rossi, the most skeptical of our respondents, now feels that values are more important than knowledge. This implicit either-or position is not necessary, however. An explicit multivariate model of the components of society would assume that now knowledge, now values, but not necessarily always the one or the other, would prevail in policy-making. Ideas, or knowledge, are important in social change, but not exclusively so.

As a result of the need for a favorable set of social and political conditions to make social research effective in social policy, it is not easy to predict when effectiveness will occur. Peck points out that none of the pro-deregulation of transportation experts meeting in the early 1970s really expected that the deregulatory actions of the CAB and the deregulatory legislation of the late 1970s would come into being so soon, if indeed ever. They could not predict the occurrence of such conducive factors as the sharp rise of inflation and the growth of the general ideology of deregulation.

It is evident from our respondents' views on effectiveness that they hold a pluralist view of society and of social and political power. They do not single out any single, overbearing center of power but are aware of the diverse values and interests that play their part in the political process. Indeed, Janowitz suggests, sometimes there is too much dispersion of power and as a result it is difficult to get Congress and the various parts of the executive branch to work together to effectuate policy. Ginzberg agrees and says that the President is not as powerful as he is often supposed to be. In a pluralist situation, Ginzberg suggests, a "crisis" is often necessary to make policy change possible.

It is also evident that our respondents would agree that social change is possible but hard. What Ginzberg calls "crises" may be what I have described as the "scandals" that made change possible in the control of experimentation on human subjects. Particularly visible and extreme examples of social problems are what may constitute felt "crises" or "scandals" and lead to a greater possibility for social change. But change also comes when some insiders in a problem situation become a force for that change. Westin, for example, refers to the existence of certain corporations that were willing early on to face up to privacy problems in the business sector and act upon his research and policy recommendations to improve the situation for their employees. I tell of medical research insiders like Dr. Henry Beecher of Harvard who, again very early on, "blew the whistle" on ethical deficiencies in biomedical research. It is not surprising that Westin has gone on to study the phenomenon of "whistle blowing" in industry and government. He would like to improve the conditions for its occurrence and protect those who practice it.

It should be noted from the cases, and this pattern is similar to many technological applications from the natural sciences, that it may take a long time before research interacts with favorable factors and becomes effective. Several of the cases report long-term *programs* of research and policy work that finally resulted in some effectiveness. Coleman, Peck, Pechman, Ginzberg, and Westin all were involved in long-term research and policy agendas. Social reform and change is often slow and hard. There must be both the necessary accumulation of social research results and the conjunction of other favorable factors for achieving the recommended policy.

One last point about social change. Many social theorists over the centuries have been aware of the unexpected consequences of deliberate social change. In recent times, Robert Merton has made the phenomenon of the "unintended consequences of purposive social change" a main and life-time theme of his theoretical work. An example of this phenomenon occurs in the Peck case. He points out that one of the unexpected consequences of the deregulation of the transportation industry has been considerable harm to a number of interests: airline employees, trucking franchise holders, and small communities now deprived of airline service. As social researchers make policy recommendations for social change, they will need to be aware of this possibility and perhaps likelihood of some unintended and undesirable side-effects.

In an activist, rational society like ours, there is considerable potential for reform and even more fundamental change. Empirical social research and social science more generally have their part to play in these potentialities. Our cases show social researchers very much disposed to take up that part. They are not technocrats, though some of them started with the conviction that they could be. They want to be part of the complex process of change along with all the other actors in a democratic and pluralist society.

Continuity

When asked, in the last of the subsets of questions, what their specific or programmatic research has led them on to, our respondents reply, not unexpectedly, since research and policy-making are endless processes, that there is, as Westin puts it, still plenty to do of both research and policy. Pechman claims some progress in understanding taxation processes and policy but, again, says that there is need for more work on both research and policy. Coleman, as indicated earlier, feels that his research has raised questions of macrosociological theory that are now at the center of his attention. And I have found that, even though I have moved on to other theoretical and research interests, I cannot "let go" in the area of biomedical ethics. I am asked to serve on ethics review committees and to give papers on this subject. There is something in the assumption that some hold that "once an expert always an expert." Of course, new researchers and policy experts may take "center stage" and former experts can withdraw to the wings.

Conclusion

Overall, the cases seem to indicate the actual and potentially important place of empirical social research for social policy in a pluralistic democracy. In the long perspective, social research as we know it today is a very recent social invention. Since World War II there has even come to be defined and institutionalized a specialty within social science called "policy research." Whether done under that label or not, effective social science now exists in some measure. Very probably it has not yet achieved the fullness of its possibilities. It has been our purpose in this book, by illustrating through specific cases the effectiveness of social research for policy and by beginning the search for the patterns and sources of that effectiveness, to help social research move a little faster in realizing its potentiality for policy effectiveness. This is a beginning, a step along the way.

Bernard Barber

The Ethics of the Use of Human Subjects in Biomedical Research (The Prototype Case)

Bernard Barber, a member of the Barnard College and graduate faculties at Columbia University, has written in the fields of sociology of science, social stratification, the sociology of knowledge, and the professions. He is primarily interested in the development of social theory and its application in empirical research of all kinds. His venture into research on the ethics of the use of human subjects in biomedical research, combined with his interest in the sociology of science, led him into the analysis presented in this essay and to the making of this book.

Written: Spring 1982

This is an account of some research by me and my colleagues on the ethics of the use of human subjects in biomedical research[1] and how it came to have some small and indirect effect on public policy. I did not start the research with any social policy effects in mind. My concern, rather, was basically theoretical, though I also had some mild egalitarian

---

[1] Bernard Barber, John J. Lally, Julia Loughlin Makarushka, and Daniel Sullivan. *Research on Human Subjects: Problems of Social Control in Medical Experimentation* (New York: Russell Sage Foundation, 1973).

and humanitarian value interests as well. I was trained in the later 1930s (undergraduate) and in the middle 1940s (graduate, with World War II having intervened) by Talcott Parsons, Robert Merton, Pitirim Sorokin, and L. J. Henderson to be a sociological theorist. I was taught to value contributions to social systems theory (the basic science relevance) more highly than those to social policy (the applied science relevance). Contributions to theory were to be made through the collection and analysis of empirical materials, not just through the construction of empty theoretical categories or through the logical manipulation of concepts and generalizations ungrounded in specific empirical measures and data.[2] Thus, very early on in my career, I did theoretical-empirical studies of such diverse topics as messianic movements among the North American Indians, activism and apathy in social systems, "fashion" in women's clothes, and the sociology of science.[3] My conviction of the importance of developing systematic theory in close conjunction with systematic empirical data was enormously strengthened in the late 1940s by my reading the work of Paul F. Lazarsfeld.[4] From him I learned about the "measurement problem" and the uses of empirical data for the construction of social theory in a clarified and systematic way that had never been available to me before. When I went to Columbia University in 1952, I went there because of my belief that it was there that social theory (as represented by Robert K. Merton) and social research (much of its new methods invented by Lazarsfeld and his associates at the newly established Bureau of Applied Social Research) were most effectively being brought together. The kind of research that my colleagues and I finally published only in 1973 on the ethics of research on human subjects was what I had hoped to do much earlier at Columbia, but those efforts were abortive.

Because of some of the theoretical/substantive concerns of my mentors, Parsons and Merton, I came to work heavily in the interwoven fields of the sociology of science, the sociology of the professions, and

---

[2] Bernard Barber. "Theory and Fact in the Work of Talcott Parsons," in Samuel Z. Klausner and Victor M. Lidz, eds., *The Nationalization of the Social Sciences* (University of Pennsylvania Press, 1986).

[3] "Acculturation and messianic movements," *American Sociological Review,* 6 (1941): 663–69; *"Mass Apathy" and Voluntary Social Participation in the United States,* doctoral dissertation, Department of Sociology, Harvard University, 1949 (New York: Arno Press, 1980); with Lyle Lobel, " 'Fashion' in women's clothes and the American social system," *Social Forces,* 31 (1952): 124–31; and *Science and the Social Order* (Glencoe, IL: Free Press, 1952).

[4] Paul F. Lazarsfeld and Morris Rosenberg, eds. *The Language of Social Research* (Glencoe, IL: Free Press, 1955).

the sociology of medicine.[5] With Renee Fox, an early student of mine and then a colleague, I did work in the area where the sociology of science and the sociology of medical research overlapped. Somewhere in the course of that work I wrote out and filed away the outline for a book on the sociology of drugs. A few years later, with Russell Sage funding, I wrote *Drugs and Society*.[6] It did not involve any new survey or field research but was a work of theoretical construction and synthesis, starting with an attempt to give a generalized definition of "a drug" and treating intensively both therapeutic drugs and the so-called dangerous or addictive drugs. During the course of writing the book, I was invited, at Brim's suggestion, to become the social scientist member of the Drug Research Board at the National Research Council in Washington, where, in the period 1966–70, I learned a great deal about social policy for the development and regulation of therapeutic drugs. Most important, a section of one of the chapters in *Drugs and Society,* "Professional Specialists: Their Functions and Problems," concerned clinical investigators. In this section I wrote a dozen pages on the problem of ethical and legal responsibility for experimentation on human beings. At the suggestion of my colleague at Columbia, Daniel Bell, one of the founding editors of *The Public Interest,* I published these pages in amended form in his journal.[7] I was thereby more visibly entered into the public policy lists. I can remember arguing in those days at the meetings of the Drug Research Board for higher standards of informed consent for medical research subjects. I can also remember similar arguments to the Board by the Commissioner for Food and Drugs, James Goddard. And, finally, I can also remember the strong resistance, on the grounds of their necessary research autonomy and their definition of the proper doctor-patient relationship, of my distinguished biomedical colleagues on the board. The social scientist, I discovered again, as I had discovered earlier in connection with my work in the sociology of science, was often not welcome to "the establishment" in biomedicine who were committed to their own definitions, values, and interests as against the different ones that the social scientist often pointed to or even spoke out for.

Despite my growing involvement in the social policy relevance of the-

[5] "Resistance by scientists to scientific discovery," *Science* 134 (1961):596–602; "Some problems in the sociology of the professions," *Daedalus* (Fall 1963):669–88; and with Renee C. Fox, "The case of the floppy-eared rabbits: an instance of serendipity gained and serendipity lost," *American Journal of Sociology* 64 (1958):126–36.
[6] New York: Russell Sage Foundation, 1967.
[7] "Experimenting with Humans," no. 6 (Winter 1967):91–102.

ory and research on the ethics of the use of human subjects, my greater
concern, by far, was still with basic science. I wanted to work out some
basic theoretical problems connected with what I called "the dilemma
of research and therapy" and with the effective self-regulation of powerful professionals.[8] Of course, I wanted to do this through some original
"Columbia-style" empirical survey research. Fortunately, the Russell
Sage Foundation was willing to underwrite this enterprise and gener-
ously supported me and my colleagues for the necessary two to three
years. One of my colleagues was a new post-doctoral researcher who
had studied with me earlier (Lally); the other two were pre-doctoral students (Makarushka and Sullivan) who got their dissertations from our
research. It was an excellent and successful team. We did two studies,
one of a national sample of some three hundred research institutions
using human subjects and the other of a sample of individual biomedical researchers using human subjects. These individual researchers
were located in two institutions, most of them in a large university hospital and medical research center and the others in a community and
teaching hospital center.

As I have suggested, funding and intellectual and moral support for
our work was a relatively easy problem. We did not have to engage in
anxious solicitation in different funding quarters. Because of the *Drugs*
book, which had sold very well, I had a good track record with the Russell Sage Foundation; social policy has always been a central concern of
the Foundation and it was clear that our research would, despite our
primary concerns, have an applied science relevance; the Foundation
appreciated good research and had the staff to make an expert evaluation of our plans and results; and we were not in need of particularly
large sums of money. (Indeed, my colleagues and I came to feel that
seldom had so much research been accomplished at so low a cost. Is
this a common feeling among researchers? I have seldom heard it expressed.) We operated in a happy atmosphere of mutual respect with
our funders; there were no differences of purpose and interest between
them and us, either when we started or, happily, when we finished.

The key value-relevant and social policy-relevant findings of our two
studies can be stated succinctly. In their responses to our "hypothetical-
factual" research protocols, the two sets of research leaders and individual researchers we studied showed a significant minority who were
what we called "permissive" with respect to the problem of the risk-

---

[8] "Control and responsibility in the powerful professions," *Political Science Quarterly*, 93
(1978–79):599–615.

benefit ratio problem posed in the protocols. Similarly, a slightly smaller minority was "permissive" with respect to the problem of informed consent for the subjects also posed in the protocols. "Permissive" and "strict" responses were defined not by some outside and absolute moral standards but only in relation to one another. When a considerable majority responded in one way about the risk-benefit ratio or about informed consent, the minority was defined as "permissive" in comparison to the "strict," those who were more concerned for the patient's welfare. We also found that the more risky studies were more likely to be done on the ward and clinic patients—that is, the poorer, less well educated, presumably less competent patients.

How does it happen that the treatment of research subjects is sometimes less than satisfactory, even in some of the most respected university and hospital research centers? Our data and analysis allowed us to point to a number of apparently causative factors. For one thing, we found that there was practically no serious concern for discussion and training of research ethics in the medical schools. Only 13 percent of our respondents reported that they had been exposed in medical school to part of a course, a seminar, or a single lecture on research ethics. A small percentage said they became aware of ethical problems in research when they did medical school training procedures on one another or when they used experimental animals. Some did remember discussion of ethical issues in connection with specific research projects. All together, 43 percent of the respondents had one or more of these ethical training experiences; the other 57 percent had not had a single one.

Another source of unsatisfactory ethics in regard to human subjects was the inadequate or altogether absent ethical peer review monitoring devices. Until 1966, only a minority of the medical research institutions and medical schools had themselves set up ethical peer review boards, and most of these were half-hearted and ineffectual. In 1966, using the power of the purse, the National Institutes of Health mandated ethical peer review committees for all institutions being funded by them. In effect, this meant all American medical research institutions, and they immediately all fell into line. However, the data collected in our first study indicated that many of these committees were ineffective, requiring no revisions of the protocols submitted to them, let alone rejecting any of them for cause. Many of the committees did not meet face to face or in any way monitor the progress of approved research.

Finally, the values, attitudes, and interests of the individual researchers in what were important qualities in their research colleagues were not such as to make ethical concerns about human subjects salient or important. When we asked our 350 individual researchers, all of whom had used human subjects, "What three characteristics do you most want to know about another researcher before entering into a collaborative relation with him?" 86 percent mentioned scientific ability, 45 percent mentioned motivation to work hard, 43 percent mentioned personality, and only 6 percent mentioned anything we could classify as "ethical concern for research subjects."

All of these findings, and more, supported the major theoretical hypothesis with which I had started, namely, that modern medical research was caught in what I called "the dilemma of science and therapy." Our researchers were powerfully constrained by their training, by their colleagues, and by the great prestige rewards possible in research to put more emphasis on science than on therapy. Often the two values could be satisfactorily accommodated to one another, but where they could not, the balance sometimes tipped toward science. One of our research findings further supported this analysis. We found that the researchers who were more likely to be doing the "permissive" studies with respect to either the risk-benefit ratio or the informed consent issues were the failed but still striving scientists, the researchers who were publishing a lot but getting no recognition either from researchers in the larger scientific community or in their local institutions. The great achievements of medical science during the last two generations have come at some ethical cost.

As our research findings emerged and as our analysis proceeded, it became clear to me that our work had definite relevance both for larger value questions and for social policy looking to the improvement of the existing situation in medical research using human subjects. Therefore, in the last chapter of our book, "The Social Responsibilities of a Powerful Profession: Some Suggestions for Policy Change and Reform," I dealt explicitly with these two kinds of relevance. After a general discussion of the relationship between the values of powerful professions in our society and the other values of that society, I described, based on the findings and analysis of our book, a set of specific social policy changes with regard to five areas: the competition structures of science and of local scientific institutions, socialization structures and processes in medical training and research institutions, collaboration groups and informal interaction structures among researchers, peer groups review, and medical schools.

Since one of the points I made in my discussion of the social responsibilities of powerful professions was that effective social control for such professions had to come in considerable measure from effective self-regulation, which was presently lacking, I hoped that medical research leaders would pay attention to our research and policy recommendations and would discuss them and perhaps take steps to put them into social practice. But that was not to be. I was invited to report our work at a few medical schools and research institutions, but mostly we were greeted with indifference and a little bit of hostility. In my own university, except for a husband-wife couple who were personal friends, not a single member of our very distinguished hospital and medical research center, which is much like the one described in our book, ever was in touch to discuss or consult with me. Whenever I could find a medical researcher sympathetic enough to listen, whenever I did describe to him or her the problems and the kind of further research that medical leaders and professional organizations might do to understand and improve the situation, the remark always was, "But we're too busy." Too busy with science, that is, with medical research on the existing ethical terms. Policy change was not going to come, in any large measure, from the inside; outside power, values, and events would have to come into play.

They did come into play, in 1973, just as our book was coming off the press, in the form of the Tuskegee medical research scandal.[9] In 1973, a journalist reported that a group of black men with syphilis in the Tuskegee, Alabama, area had been the subjects since the early 1930s of an experiment in which their disease was left untreated and they were continuously observed, all without any serious attempt at getting their informed consent. Moreover, the study continued even after 1945, when penicillin became available as the drug of choice for the treatment of the disease.

We should note that even before 1973, in the sixties, two other scandals over the treatment of human research subjects had occurred, but none had quite the large effect that the Tuskegee scandal was to have. One of the scandals involved the injection of live cancer cells into a number of geriatric patients at a hospital in Brooklyn, New York, without their informed consent. Another involved a leading virologist who conducted an experiment at Willowbrook, a New York State institution for the mentally retarded. Reasoning that a serious liver infection, hepatitis, was in effect endemic in the hospital anyway, he deliberately exposed some children to hepatitis virus in an attempt to achieve controlled conditions for testing an antihepatitis vaccine. No adequate in-

[9]James H. Jones, *Bad Blood* (New York: Free Press, 1981).

formed consent was given by administrators at Willowbook. We should note, in connection with the general significance of scandals for social change, that all of the major legislative reforms in U.S. drug regulation since the beginning of this century have occurred in connection with scandals. For example, the Kefauver-Harris Amendments of 1962 were passed only as a result of the thalidomide scandal.

For reasons which are not entirely clear, but perhaps because the Tuskegee experiment involved black people, perhaps because there was in the early 1970s a more powerful sense for civil rights in general, and probably because Senator Edward Kennedy, one of whose chief concerns has always been medical problems and rights, took the matter very seriously, the Tuskegee scandal did have considerable effects on public awareness of the human experimentation problem and on new institutional arrangements for its study and amelioration. Senator Kennedy's attention to the matter produced powerful publicity, political force, and eventual results for a new social policy.

When I heard that Senator Kennedy was to hold hearings of the Senate Health Committee on the Tuskegee scandal, I knew that our findings and analysis were relevant and I determined to try to bring them to bear. Fortunately, I had personal connections that eventually led to an invitation to testify at the Senate hearings. A couple of years before I had been approached for help by Professor Jay Katz, psychoanalyst and member of the Yale Law School faculty, who was compiling an encyclopedic collection of materials on experimentation with human subjects. I introduced him to the staff at the Russell Sage Foundation; not only did they support his work but eventually published it.[10] By chance, a physician trained at Yale who had taken a course with Katz in the Law School was now the chief medical staff person for Senator Kennedy. Katz told him about our research; both Katz and I were invited to make statements to Senator Kennedy's Committee hearings.

On March 8, 1973, in the first of Senator Kennedy's Senate Sub-Committee on Health Hearings on the problems of human experimentation, the main concern was with the Tuskegee victims themselves; some of them and their lawyers were present and testified. My invited task was to speak to the question of whether the problems revealed at Tuskegee were general in human experimentation. Reporting our research findings about the differential treatment of poor and well-to-do patients and subjects and about the defects in the actual functioning of peer review committees, I affirmed the view that these problems were indeed gen-

[10] *Experimentation with Human Beings* (New York: Russell Sage Foundation, 1972).

eral. I then went on to "strongly recommend that there be federal legislation of the use of humans in medical experimentation" because the "biomedical research profession has simply failed to take the initiative in effective self-regulation in this area" and too often leaned toward the science side of the science-humane therapy dilemma posed for biomedical science by those two competing values. I suggested the establishment of "a National Board of Biomedical Research Ethics" and gave recommendations, from the policy chapter of our book, on how such a board should be constituted and proceed.

On June 28, 1973, when I testified again, the issue before the Sub-Committee was no longer just the Tuskegee scandal but general reform legislation, the Protection of Human Subjects Act, which included provision for the establishment of a National Commission for the Protection of Human Subjects. I directed my brief testimony to three essential questions. First, in answer to the question of whether there was need for control and regulation, I repeated our findings that showed such need. Second, concerning the question of whether the proposed bill promised "to improve, significantly, present and future practice in the use of human subjects in research," I again answered in the affirmative, saying that the commission would give public visibility and raise the level of consciousness about the problem and furthermore would have the members and staff to acquire the knowledge and make the policy recommendations necessary for improving the situation. I specified some of the kinds of research the proposed commission's staff ought to be looking into. Finally, I answered yes to the third question: Is government regulation necessary? "I think so," I said, "because it is a fact, carefully demonstrated by our research findings, that the research professions have not taken the initiatives necessary for protecting their human subjects. They have tended to respond, and then reluctantly, to Government mandate enforced by the power of the purse. They have been laggard in improving the ethical education of their students, undistinguished in using peer review to control questionable research, and relatively more interested in the demands of scientific achievement than in the obligations of humane treatment of subjects."

Senator Kennedy's bill was passed and the National Commission not only was established but had an important influence on policy and practice during the next half-dozen years, eventually to be succeeded by a President's Commission for the general area of biomedical ethics, including a whole range of problems beyond human experimentation such as *in vitro* fertilization, the distribution of health services, and the like. Surely the effects of our research findings on social policy through the establishment of the commission were small; Senator Kennedy's great moral and political power were what carried the day in the face of considerable professional and political opposition; but I was convinced that our research and recommendations had been relevant and perhaps useful.

My influence on the commission did not stop with its establishment. I continued to have a small influence in a number of ways. My research associate, Bradford Gray, who had himself done excellent participant observation research on the shortcomings of the informed consent and peer review processes for human experimentation, became the staff sociologist to the commission and introduced a continuing sociological research tradition into its work.[11] I served on one of the commission's advisory committees for the award of a research contract that was mandated by the bill establishing the commission. The mandated research was much too inclusive and diffuse, I thought, but eventually was awarded by the staff of the commission, against the advice of its advisory committee, to a poor contractor. Finally, along with many others, I was asked to prepare an advisory paper; my topic was the role of assessment of risk/benefit criteria in the determination of the appropriateness of research involving human subjects.[12] Thus, in a variety of ways, I had some small continuing influence with the commission because I had been defined by our research as a social science researcher authority on experimentation. I probably would have had more influence except that the commission, partly because of the affiliations and preferences of its members, partly because of those of its staff and advisers, leaned more heavily to moral philosophy and moral theology than to social science research as the basis for its discussions and policy recommendations. This is a general characteristic of the biomedical ethics area. Nevertheless, both the commission and the biomedical ethics movement have been responsible for considerable improvement in the treatment of human subjects in research.

The influence of our research on policy was not limited to the government level. At the Ford Foundation, for their programs of grants for research in reproductive biology, I assisted in the construction of a policy for the ethical practices of all grantees using human subjects and continued as ethics consultant to that program for several years. My association with the Ford Foundation involved considerable experience

[11] Bradford H. Gray. *Human Subjects in Medical Experimentation* (New York: Wiley, 1975).
[12] Published in National Commission for the Protection of Human Subjects, *The Belmont Report*, 3 vols. (Washington, DC: U.S. Government Printing Office, 1978).

with the special problems of biomedical researchers outside the United States, both in the Third World and in quite different societies like Japan and India. In addition to my work for the Ford Foundation, I served, first as member and then as chairman for some years, of the Human Subjects Review Committee, the local peer review committee at Columbia University, for all nonmedical research using human subjects. Here I was able to apply some of our research and policy perspectives and even did a little informal research on the committee's decisions and experiences which I reported in my risk/benefit paper for the National Commission. I have maintained continuing knowledge of the peer review process through continued contact, after my membership, with the Human Subjects Review Committee. This contact is also maintained by my serving as an advisory editor of *IRB,* a valuable publication on the problems of peer review committees, edited by Robert Levine of Yale and sponsored by the Hastings Center.[13]

Beyond these more or less direct influences of our research on government and organizational policy, multiple channels and modes of influence were opened during the next few years and thereafter. Our book was distributed by the Russell Sage Foundation to a considerable number of notables and influentials both in general and in the medical policy field specifically. I never perceived any results from that effort, though there may have been some. More important for getting attention for our work and establishing me as an authority on our subject was a very favorable review of our book by Professor David Mechanic, a leading researcher and policy adviser in medical sociology, in *Science,* the prestigious and widely read weekly magazine of the American Association for the Advancement of Science. Perhaps even more important for getting our work attention and establishing our authority was an article I was asked to contribute to *Scientific American,* the premier general science magazine.[14] Based on this article, reports on our research, findings, and policy recommendations appeared in the *New York Times,* in newspapers throughout the country, and in other media.

Other modes of influence that were opened by our research included consulting with public interest advocacy groups, advising administrative decision-makers, speaking at special-interest group and professional meetings and conferences, counseling others who were writing about the problems of human experimentation in biomedicine, training stu-

---

[13] Robert J. Levine, *Ethics and Regulation of Clinical Research* (Baltimore: Urban and Schwarzenberg, 1981).
[14] "The ethics of experimentation with human subjects," vol. 234, no. 2 (1975):25–31.

dents and giving advice on further research in this field, and generally
becoming an information center and intermediary among researchers
and policy activists with interests related to ours. As a sociologist of science looking for the patterns of our influence on social policy, I began
to keep a detailed log of my activities. The following selected specifics
from this log for the years 1973 to 1975 (when activities increased
heavily because of the *Scientific American* article) illustrate the various
modes of influence I could apply to public awareness and social policy:

February 1973: consultation on their report with a member of the
Tuskegee Syphilis Study Ad Hoc Committee appointed by the Secretary
of Health, Education, and Welfare.

March 1973: attendance at the conference on research ethics sponsored by MedCom, a consulting firm for the ethical pharmaceutical industry; consultation with legal counsel representing Law and Social Policy, a public interest law group representing candidates for psychosur-
gery who were on public welfare in Michigan.

April 1973: attendance at the Smithsonian Institution Conference on
Human Experimentation; talk to the Due Process Committee of the National American Civil Liberties Union on the same subject; lecture to
faculty and undergraduates at Ramapo College, New Jersey; lecture to a
group at the University of Kansas Medical School at the invitation of a
sympathetic member of the faculty.

May 1973: consultation with the Kennedy Foundation for Mental Re-
tardation on proposed legislation on medical experimentation.

July 1973: Columbia College undergraduate radio and newspaper interviews.

August 1973: interview with *Medical Tribune,* a widely distributed international medical news and policy newspaper.

September 1973: consultation with a staff member of the American
Bar Foundation proposing to do research on ethical peer review
groups.

January 1974: consultation with a staff writer for *Science Digest* on an
article on human experimentation; consultation with *Consumer Reports*
on an article on the ethics of overseas drug research; consultation with
a staff member of the Children's Defense Fund, Washington, on problems of research on children.

February 1974: appearance on WOR-TV, New York; talk to the Research Council, New York City Chapter of the National Association of
Social Workers; talk to Professor William Curran's law and ethics group
at the Harvard School of Public Health.

March 1974: consultation with Alex Gordon, who was writing an article for *Physician's World* on behavioral modification experiments on prisoners.

May 1974: consultation with Dr. Richard Restak, a neurologist from Washington, writing a book on bioethics which, when published, described our work.

May–June 1974: correspondence and discussion with Dr. Arthur M. Sackler, publisher of *Medical Tribune* about his three articles describing and criticizing our research.

June 1974: consultation with Sylvia Chase of CBS for the Walter Cronkite show, about pending legislation in Congress, fetal research, and so forth; also consultation with Steve Steinberg of CBS about special show on human experimentation.

Throughout this period: publication of book reviews on bioethics and human experimentation in such journals as *Political Science Quarterly, Minerva,* and *American Journal of Orthopsychiatry.*

November 1974: Sigma Xi Lecture to Olin research chapter in New Haven; participation in Harvard University interdisciplinary bioethics seminar.

December 1974: lecture at the Department of Sociology, University of Chicago; talk at a general university meeting, Columbia University; invited lecture at the annual meeting of American Association for Neuropsychopharmacology, Puerto Rico.

January 1975: Sigma Xi Lecture, Texaco Research Laboratory, Beacon, New York; talk to Nutrition Studies Section, National Institutes of Health; talk to Doctor of Medical Science Program, Downstate Medical Center, Brooklyn, New York; chairman and arranger, session on ethics of research, national meeting of American Association for the Advancement of Science, New York.

February 1975: participation, forum on bioethics, National Academy of Sciences, Washington.

March 1975: as consultant to Ford Foundation, discussions on human experimentation with researchers in India and Philippines.

April 1975: paper on the ethics of behavioral research experimentation at the Eastern Psychological Association.

May 1975: consultation with a staff member of the National Commission; participation, Social Science Research Council meeting on ethics of social research; consultation with a staff member of the National Institutes of Health about possible intramural program on ethics of research.

June 1975: participation, Advisory Board, Bureau of Social Science Research, Washington, study of ethics of social research; member, evaluation panel, National Commission, proposals for mandated special study of ethical issues in research; member, advisory committee, Balter-Mellinger study of public attitudes toward risk/benefit and informed consent issues in biomedical research.

September 1975: consultation, journalist writing article for national magazine on bioethics; invitation, House Judiciary Committee, testimony on legislation banning use of prisoners in research; lecture, Scientific Advisory Council, Distilled Spirits Association; consultant, Code of Ethics of American College of Neuropsychopharmacology; consultation, for speech, president of Association for Advancement of Behavior Therapy.

October 1975: consultation, graduate student of David Mechanic's at Wisconsin, on doing Ph.D. research on bioethics topic; discussion, Professor Eliot Valenstein, on ethics of research in brain control research field.

As the details of this log make evident, there were a considerable number and variety of modes and opportunities for our research to have influence on public knowledge and public policy about the ethics of research on human subjects. Compared with the situation as it had existed in this country as late as the 1960s, there has been slow but considerable improvement in the ethical treatment of human research subjects. Nevertheless, there remains room for further improvement; the glass is now half-full, but it is also still half-empty. Improvements are still possible and desirable with regard to professional attitudes toward the ethical problems of research, with regard to satisfactory ethical training for medical researchers and therapists, and perhaps especially with regard to more effective self-regulation of professional researchers through the local peer review and other formal and informal social control mechanisms.

Improvement has been slower than it might otherwise have been because of the continuing strong resistance of many powerful professionals to findings and recommendations like ours. Some of these professionals have persisted in seeing the problem as minor or even negligible, as a matter of individualistic psychological or moral defect ("a few bad apples"), not as a matter of a defective social system of training and control. Others, standing absolutistically on the scientific and professional value of autonomy for themselves in their research and practice, have resented and resisted all efforts at regulatory reform, even when the new regulations were to be administered by their peers. Some have been unwilling to acknowledge that nonprofessionals, citizens in general, have their own strong interest and value stake in professional power and its effects, much of it for good, but also for ill in some respects.

Resistance to adjusting values to one another, to regulatory reform, has by no means been limited to biomedical researchers. As government regulations and peer review requirements were extended to social and behavioral research, some social scientists, and especially the researchers among them using human subjects, such as the experimental social psychologists, have become even more vehement critics of peer review. For example, on general value grounds, Professor Ithiel Pool, a political scientist at the Massachusetts Institute of Technology, made himself a very active, visible, and passionate critic of peer review as "prior restraint" and as a violation of First Amendment freedoms.

Such resistance from biomedical and social science researchers is to be expected. Research findings such as ours did have strong implications for fundamental values, for those of scientific autonomy, on the one hand, and for those of equality and humane therapy, on the other. Our findings did imply that there might be a change in the existing balance or emphasis on these different values; it did imply, and we recommended accordingly, some changes in social policy. When strong values are at issue and when social policy changes based on these values are recommended, as they have been here, then resistance by powerful groups is to be expected.

This expectable resistance by powerful groups with strong value commitments, to research findings implying social policy changes affecting their values and practices, is only one of the *general* lessons I have learned in a new way as a result of my research and policy experience with the problem of experimentation on human subjects. I guess I always knew it in the abstract, but now I know it in a concrete and affect-laden way. Never again will I expect, as I think I did at the beginning of this research, that the powerful group under scrutiny will be objective and pay attention to the results of research on their behavior and quickly take action to remedy readily apparent shortcomings.

Another *general* lesson learned, closely interrelated with the first one, is that social reform and social change are very likely to be hard and slow. New knowledge will usually have a hard time making its way; it will have to be sent through many channels to many individual and group actors in the social system. Those social researchers who start out with or develop along the way commitment to new social policy and social change need to learn this lesson if they are going to be prepared for and tolerant of the long and hard road they will have to travel.

Finally, so far as the relations between social science research and social policy are concerned, our research has taught me a solid lesson in the complex and multiple various possible relations between them. The researcher can start with one or the other and move to its opposite either by design or in some unexpected and unintended fashion. They are both independent and interdependent; that is, each has its own standards and procedures but each also has some consequences for the other. No simple scientific or moral reductionism is possible in treating of the relations between social research and social policy.

Is this the end of my story? No, the tale continues. Our research having established me as an expert and the "social problems" of bioethics having continued to be of governmental and public policy import, I have found that I cannot "let go." Both in my work and in my policy activities, my past continues into the present. On the policy and activities side many of the kinds of specifics detailed above in my log for 1973–75 continue right into the present, though at a diminished rate because of some general slowdown in this area and because of my own wish to turn my attention elsewhere. On the research and writing side, I have to some degree extended my concern with bioethics, to some degree focused my attention on more general sociological problems underlying the particulars of this area: thus, "Control and responsibility in the powerful professions", *Informed Consent in Medical Therapy and Research,* and *The Logic and Limits of Trust.*[15] In these different works, the value-relevance and the policy-relevance and the social science knowledge-relevance are all there, though with somewhat different emphasis in the different cases. Probably the emphasis, because of my own stronger values, always goes more heavily to the knowledge and theory relevance. But values and policy are never far off.

---

[15]*Political Science Quarterly,* 93 (1978–79), 599–615; (New Brunswick, NJ: Rutgers University Press, 1980); and (New Brunswick, NJ: Rutgers University Press, 1983).

Index